MGH

God Lifted Me: Lessons of My Lifetime, A Book of Poems

First published by Inspiring Honey Publishing, LLC ; Funky Fresh Nerd Imprint 2023

Library of Congress Number Applied For.

First edition

ISBN: 979-8-218-23186-6

Editing by Dr. Tiffany Jones-Fisher
Cover art by Alexandria Cunningham

This book was professionally typeset on Reedsy.
Find out more at reedsy.com

To Larry Lee and Mary Catherine, thank you for loving me enough to expect nothing less than the best of me, and when I fell short, for loving me even more because you knew it was not from a lack of trying. My heart misses you, but my soul rejoices in your rest.

Contents

Foreword

"God Lifted Me" is written to give my Heavenly Father, the Holy Spirit, and Jesus Christ all the glory, honor, praise, and gratitude my soul can muster. The poems reflect personal healing, affirmation and validation. For five years, I have been bound by loss and grief, and I never knew it until I decided to be obedient and walk in the fullness of my purpose. I have been a writer of sorts since I was a teenager. However, I temporarily allowed a creative writing course to derail my writing future. When I consider those I could have touched or helped during my time of disobedience, I am ashamed and repentant. I am humbled that God lifted me and uses me as a vessel to help others through written and spoken words.

I sincerely hope the words written on these pages will uplift the minds, hearts, and spirits of those who read them. And yes, it is my goal to challenge the readers. I want them to think beyond themselves and focus on the purpose of being here. None of us are here to merely take up space. None of us are worthless or hapless beings. Transforming our minds, hearts, and spirits takes work. And for me, it takes constant, daily self-reflection and meditation. Desires are real. Life is tough. We were built to be tougher. We were given a how-to-manual to help us in our times of feeling defeated.

What happens when you don't know that you are lost, defeated, depressed, or anxious? Thank goodness for me; prayer and talks with God are a part of my life. They are habits for me regardless of my circumstance. I thought I had it going on for a moment, but I was clueless. When my mother died in 2017, I felt such sorrow that I didn't realize that my grieving process had stalled, and I did not mourn her absence until almost four years later. The events of 2020 in the United States of America brought my best friend, Brittina Renae Moore, back into my life. Her presence and our conversations led to the renewal of my spirit. Her invitation to go on her Facebook Live broadcast, *"Something to Say with B. Renae,"* and have honest discussions about living day-to-day life as black women and the reality of what we face daily was a wake-up call for me. I am an introvert and a private person. Expressing my opinions, which I have many, is not something I do lightly or publicly. But there was too much going on in the world around us and too much at stake for me to remain quiet and stay in my comfort zone. I had built an invisible fortress around myself and didn't want to let anyone into it. I still struggle with this. But whether I wanted to or not, the outside world disrupted my daily routine, sanity, and order in my social and work life. Something had to give because I was beginning to feel something I had never experienced: anxiety and uneasiness about my children's future.

God used my best friend's presence to lift me from my grief. I had no idea that I was functioning at half capacity. I was a decent mother. As a wife, I probably left something to be desired. I was managing a successful nursing program. But I was a fraction of the person I was born to be. I was not living in my purpose or God's will. Brittina's presence challenged me to think critically, not just about my immediate surroundings but the broader community and the world through which I am traveling as a pilgrim. Instead of complaining about what was happening, how was I helping? In this self-reflection, this questioning of my self-righteous indignation, I often thought of my youth and my love of writing. I was certain that I could not create a rhyme if I tried. I was afraid to sit in front of the computer and try to write a poem. Why? The fear of failure and disappointment was too much. I also told myself life was too busy for silly nonsense like writing poetry or children's books. I had a full-time job and a full-time family. But by 2021, as the mother of two black teenagers constantly questioning their place in the country of their birth and their ability to succeed in the world, I knew I had to do something.

I was also the leader of a nursing program of majority African American students on campus with young ladies who may need help from a professional mentor. I sat down at my computer and I typed. About an hour later, I was staring at the words in "Mirror, Mirror". Mind you; I said I typed it.

The words came quicker than I could type. They were the sincere words of a heart and spirit of gratitude for those who lived before me and overcame great obstacles. They were words of assurance that I could achieve all that I was born to accomplish, and I have plenty of role models in history to remind me of that, not the least of which is my mother.

One thing I have learned about the God I serve: He will bring you to doors, but He will NOT force you to walk through them. Faith must show up. We must be willing to walk through the door or at least take the first step. I sat at the computer and started typing (my first step). My gift, that's how I see it, had only left me for a season. In actuality, it had not left me at all. It merely lay dormant until I decided to use it. Do you have a gift that is lying dormant? Here is the truly amazing part. After I wrote "Mirror, Mirror," my mind would not shut off. Rhymes bombarded my brain at all times of the day. I read "Mirror, Mirror" in one of our Sustah2Sister seminars on campus. A colleague and now friend, Dr. B.J. Kimbrough, approached me after the meeting and said, "You have a gift. People need to see this."

Furthermore, she told me she knew a publisher. She was my validation, my confirmation. And this time, I was not going to be disobedient. Hence, the book you are now reading.

Please consider your unique purpose, your unique self. Self-reflection and awareness are essential. You are here for a reason; and good enough to fulfill your purpose. We all have desires. We are all dealing with ourselves daily and trying to become better versions of ourselves. I am not exempt. I had to learn to, and am still learning to, rely on faith. But don't forget that faith, without work, is dead. Enjoy the poems. Some are to challenge you and help you grow. Some are playful and meant to bring a smile to your heart, mind, or spirit. Some are to remind you that I am human and a woman. In all of them, I am certain that nothing can remove me from the love of God. I pray that you know that, too. Where relevant, I have added a scripture verse or verses that coincide with my thought process while writing.

And So, It Begins...

Reliving the past
   It only makes the pain last
   So long, I lived in a shell

Friendship departed
   Now broken-hearted
   My private version of hell

Daddy died, barely made it.
   This new life, starting to hate it
   The me I once knew no longer exists

Oh my God, now Mama's gone
   Surrounded by people but on my own
   I'm so defeated. Please help me get through this.

Children keeping me in the game
   Lord, please remember my name
   I know there is work for me to do here

Didn't bring me this far to leave me
   The enemy, man, he has deceived me
   Please come and save me, Jesus for this my prayer.

Psalm 27

Affirmation

He speaks to me every morning
  Whispers gently in my ear
  It's time for the day to begin
  I'm with you, always near. Do not fear.

He washes me with rays of the sun
  Kisses my skin with His gentle wind
  Or sends His rain to wash away
  My sins, so I may, once again, begin.

He graces me with His presence.
  The ability to see me through His eyes.
  He allows me to be who I am when I'm with Him
  Never asking me to disguise or compromise.

Though I judge myself so harshly
  And I make mistake after mistake
  He listens to me confess every night
  Yet, still reappears when I wake.

He is patiently giving guidance.
  Without forcing me to abide by His laws
  He has the power to make me submit
  But He believes in me with all my flaws.

He believes that I will get it right
   Learn to walk within my purpose.
   Despite imperfections
   He tells me that my true self will one day surface.

For those who seek affirmation and validation
   As we all so often do
   Imagine being affirmed and validated
   By the One who created you.

I remind myself every day.
   That all these words are true
   With God for me, who holds all power
   There is nothing His daughter cannot do.

Romans 8:31

Alternate Universe

Is living in an alternate universe
   My sincere blessing or my untimely curse

Each day that I wake
   I think how normal the day will be
   But then I make a fatal mistake
   I turn on the TV

Tornadoes, volcanoes, wars
   Shooting sprees everywhere
   Politicians unqualified to do the people's business
   Man, I swear

I want to shout
   To the top of my lungs to scream
   Knowing they'll think I'm the one who's crazy
   See me as being obscene

Maybe they're not wrong
   And my thoughts are twisted and distorted
   Maybe that's why nothing makes sense
   Why is hatred being rewarded

Maybe I have it completely backward

And love is not stronger than hate
Daily I see people ripped to shreds
Spit in the face of that love/hate debate

Selfishness is what every person
Seems to strive for
After all, it comes so easy
It lives at our very core

And we should always do what comes easy
For hard work brings nothing to bare
Only suffering, begging, and misunderstanding
All the pain we can spare

I've had it all wrong in my head
I should've been putting myself first
That's the only way to get ahead
And survive the alternate universe

But my spirit rebukes these thoughts
Of a world where love is at fault
A world where kindness, meekness, and compassion
All are under assault

Try as I might to fit into this space
Where complacent self-indulgence abides
My heart, my mind, my soul will not let me rest
They reject it. They won't backslide.

Instead of turning a blind eye to wrongdoing
And pretending I know all the answers
I try to understand other's points of view
My temptations I try to master

Alt U, the place where I live on the daily
  It takes every ounce of my sanity to survive
  With God's grace, mercy, love, and much prayer
  In this world, I am managing to thrive

Matthew 24:4-13

Begin with Me

You want to see a sinner
  You can begin with me
  You want to see a winner
  Again, look my way and see

You want to see a frightened girl
  You can begin with me
  You want to see one who's hated this world
  Then gaze at me wonderingly

You want to see a quitter
  You can begin with me
  One who, at times has felt quite bitter
  Yep, I'm afraid it's me you'd see

You want to see a humble soul
  You can begin with me
  One who thanks God I learned before I was old
  I'll show myself gladly

You want to see a perfect being
  You must turn and look elsewhere
  You see, I am for the seeing
  Of those with eyes willing to be made aware

You want to see perfection
  That lies in none of us, not one
  My imperfections, I've got a collection
  The one you seek, well, that's God's son

You want to see the ones He loves
  You can begin with me
  Forget the imperfections I spoke of
  Jesus still loves me, you see

You want me to tell you He's no need for you
  No, do not begin with me
  For I know the truth of what my God can do
  No difference He makes; you'll see

You want to see someone just like you
  You can begin with me
  In my Father's house, not knowing what to do
  Feeling uncomfortable and unworthy

You want to see someone who would not be denied
  You can begin with me
  Messing up and acting out, all along I cried
  Dear God, You have to be

You want to see someone who knows His voice
  You can begin with me
  Lost and alone, left without a choice
  He lifted me and now I am free

Psalm 40:2

Beyond the Facade

Look beyond the facade
   You'll see my rod
   He's standing there
   If I lay me bare
   If I come clean
   You'll see the King
   You give me praise
   Yet it's all His ways
   All good and perfect
   Watch Him work it
   Through me, His vessel
   No need to wrestle
   All battles He fights
   If I just sit tight
   Be still and wait
   All fears will abate
   Don't mean to boast
   But you must look close
   Look beyond what you see
   He lives in me

1 Corinthians 6:19; John 14:15-17

BOW

I see you in the sky
   A reminder of a promise long ago
   As beautiful as you are rare
   The unique and brilliant bow

Constantly appearing
   After God cleanses us anew
   Washing the Earth with mystical rain
   Leaving behind drops of dew

High above us all
   Your majesty reigns in the sky as though
   You are inviting us to enter
   Into His presence underneath your glow

All my years looking skyward
   At times feeling so alone
   Never thought a day would come
   When I'd be blessed with my very own

Genesis 9:13-16

Brevity

The key to longevity
    Simple brevity

Doing what is easy
    Will not appease me

Try the uncomfortable
    Unlock something wonderful

You want me to be brief
    Wrap up in love, lounge in peace

Short and sweet
    No need to repeat.

Building Your House

I laid a foundation for you
    As your mother I was supposed to
    It wasn't fair to allow you into the night
    And not prepare you for the coming fight

Born without a plan and no direction
    The object of my hope and affection
    Not willing to let you tread a path unguided
    Knowing your attention would be torn and divided

Watching you grow and learn to use your voice
    Instructing you on how to make a wise choice
    Love, grace, and mercy are the discerning tools
    I placed in your kit to resist the bribery of fools

Your popularity is not what you need to build your name
    Education and faithfulness are your claim to fame
    Building your character to seek the living fountain
    Preparing you to go over, around, and through life's mountains

The materials I supplied to you as a child were crucial
    Throughout your entire life, I hope you'll find them useful
    Rejecting the tainted trappings of every nation
    That will tempt you and seek to destroy your firm foundation

Listen carefully, understand the words that I say
  Your life is too precious for me to let you "find" your way
  Without giving you building blocks with which to play
  This game called life. Use them well I pray.
  For the foundation was purposed for your parents to lay
  So, you could build a house that would stand firm one day.

Matthew 7:24-27

Buried Deep

Psst, are you here? Perhaps asleep?
　I know that you are there. Inside. Buried deep.

It has been a long time. I miss the sound of your voice.
　And, yes, I know that to leave you was my selfish choice.

I would like a chance to try to explain.
　What I was going through, the essence of my pain.

I know you understand. You were there too.
　I shouldn't have to describe what we both went through.
　How I shut you out to try to protect you.

My childhood, my youth.
　The fullness of me (Penny), my truth.

The free-spirited one, fun-loving dancer
　The inquisitive one, always looking for an answer

The lover of people, waiting for her chance
　To know her lover's touch, to feel the fire from his glance

The naïve girl who was often corrected
　She wasn't ready for the world; you needed to be protected

So, I hid you as I should, no one else was gonna
    In the shadows I hid "Penny", and took on "Mary's" persona

But I miss having you as a part of my life. I want you back now.
    Life's too serious and lonely. How do I get you back? How?!!

I miss your laughter and silliness and the way you would dream
    The way you danced around rooms and would sing to anything

Please come back and let your spirit show again
    I was wrong to hide you, to not let you in

We can both exist in the world as we know it
    I now know that I was wrong. I don't have to be afraid to show it.

Jeremiah 23:24

Cancel Me, Please

Your goal is to ostracize
  Hope it leads to my demise

Sure, hold me accountable for my words
  I uttered them when I should have deferred

I should be held responsible for my bad deeds
  Next time, I may consider myself, take heed

But to cancel me from my entire culture
  And I'm the one considered a vulture?

Want me to be removed from my job
  And I'm the one labeled a snob?

Want me to tumble and take a fall?
  Great way to model for us all!

Want to be the morality police?
  Then do the most and say the least.

Model the behavior you want exhibited
  Be the change, looks like you twisted it

Do two wrongs always make things right?
    No, the war you wage will make men fight.

Or even worse make them put on a front
    Fake, pretend to give you what you want.

Do all you can to bring me to my knees
    Makes no difference to me; cancel me, please.

John 8:7-8

Chaos

I see you, but you already know I do
   Actually, I see straight through you
   I know your minions
   All their opinions

Not happy unless balance is destroyed
   My thoughts distracted, me perpetually annoyed

The love, the joy, and happiness, you hide
   Beneath greed, and lust, and envy, and pride
   Wrapped in gossip and smiles, warm hugs and kisses
   Consuming your targets, your aim rarely misses

Chaos, you are everywhere I turn
   My dear, when will you learn?
   You no longer have control over me
   I have the antidote to your disruption of my peace

I live with you because I must
   But in the One who controls you, I trust
   There are limits to you, and that makes you weak
   And so, to me, you are obsolete

I must be about the business in my mind

And you, Chaos, are only good for wasting time
So, when I command you to get behind
You have no choice but to fall in line

Keep doing what it is you do — your duty
I know your secret, the way you hide true beauty
My task simply to pull from without
Those souls for which you are busy casting doubt

Chaos, I see your immense ocean
Tempted to drink from your sweet potion
But, refuse to satisfy your alluring call
That will lead to my destruction and ensuing downfall

I Corinthians 14:33

Choose Me

All my life I wanted to be someone's number one
　Tired of being looked over, through with it, done.

When you came along I thought my time had come
　Finally, I'm the first, second to none

The apple of your eye; your pie in the sky
　The shoulder you'd run to whenever you needed to cry

All those dumb clichés that would make me the center
　Your beginning and your end, your warmth in the dead of winter

I knew that finally I had found the one to place me at his side
　As time passed on, I realized that to myself I'd lied

My fate is not to be the center of any man's universe
　Instead, my lot is centered on learning to put me first

Taking time to care for me so that I may care for them
　Taking stresses off myself, removing pressure off of him

Accepting that it is ok to make my happiness
　Not wallow in a made-up world that causes much distress

Is this an acceptable place to be
   Living in a world where I choose me

I can love you and love me too and accept each as we are
   Lay down my weapons and choose to love, in peace, not hate in war.

Romans 12:1-2

Creator

I've considered Venus, the moon, the sun
   The lesser stars in the sky
   I've wondered if we, man, have remained
   The apple of Your eye. If so, why?

The greatest of all Your creations
   In Your image was made
   To care for all of creation
   Not allow any to fade

Defiant in our knowledge and love for self
   Lost in our lust, our greed, our desire
   In love with the world's money and flesh
   Our insatiable hunger feeds the fire

Your love is kind and faithful to us
   We act as though it's never enough
   Always asking and expecting from you
   Never reciprocal, what must we do
   Don't we play a role in this, too
   In honoring You
   Our forever True
   Creator.
   Isaiah 40: 27-31; 1 Corinthians 10:31

Crown Shifters, Not Allowed

On the day of my birth,
    It seems I forgot my worth,
    My crown invisible for the naked "I" to see

As I grew up as a child,
    Somehow I knew, all the while,
    That royal blood was inevitably a part of me

From humble beginnings I came
    At least, that is the refrain
    In the sight of man who walks this Earth aimlessly

As he seeks to find his fame
    Seeks, on Earth, to make his name
    I was given to know all these things would be added unto me

It would seem that time and man
    Through their misguided plan
    Worked hard to ensure the rewriting of my fate

But little did they know
    They would only help me grow
    Redeeming the crown on my head that refused to be tilted by hate

And while at times I feel undeserving
    And the weight of the crown is unnerving
    I feel it shift upon my head when tempted; I swear it weighs a ton

But, then I reflect upon my past
    Through my invisible looking glass
    And, with a gentle sigh I erect my crown so I may show others how it is
done

Because I choose to rise above
    Because I choose to love
    Crown-shifters must understand that the battle has already been WON!

Overtime, through the span of my life
    Evil hoped to make me sacrifice
    The beautiful crown adorned perfectly on my head since my birth

For those who wear your crown
    Never hang your head down
    Crown-shifters are not allowed, only YOU DETERMINE YOUR WORTH.

Proverbs 4:5-9; Luke 12:6-7; 1 Peter 2:9

Deep Sleep

Tossing, turning
   Moaning, groaning
   In my dreams
   You won't stop roaming

On the couch on the floor
   On my back, on my side
   Going with you
   On an erotic ride

Shouldn't be here
   I don't behave like this
   You won't let me talk
   Distracting me with your kiss

Thrust after thrust
   The river flows freely
   Shhh…must be quiet
   Can't let anyone see me

Can't believe the sounds
   So loud and so wild
   Carrying me to the bed
   I hold on tight all the while

The moves once fast
　　Now masterfully slow
　　Telling me soon
　　That you'll have to let go

I hold on tighter
　　My thighs spreading wider
　　Tempting you to stay with me
　　The alarm clock sounds
　　And as I look around
　　I'm alone and back in my reality

Disclaimers

All our lives we've heard we could be what we wanted
    Almost weekly the words in front of us were flaunted
    But what exactly are the seeds being daily planted
    In the minds of the youth that they're taking for granted

Sure, they have gifts that will allow them to start
    In any career that they choose to take part
    And yes they have means to obtain the education
    To open doors to place them in the best situation

But what of the disclaimers that they must be willing
    To have a work ethic that will gain them top billing
    For it takes more than "want-to" to climb the ladder
    The ability to do their due diligence has to matter

Everyone will show up, but who will stand out
    Not all privy to hook-ups, not all born with clout
    You must be willing to combine your talents with intellect
    Because faith without works is easy to detect

Many want to, but aren't willing to do what it takes
    Study long, show up early, and good times forsake
    Let's be honest when we tell them they can be anything
    Read the small print, the disclaimer: only if your best you are willing to

bring

James 2:14

Distraction

Mind starting to roam
   In all the wrong directions
   Need to be about work
   Body making other suggestions

Thinking of things, I could do
   To make it on the naughty list
   Trying hard to stay focused
   But parts of my anatomy, they persist

What can I do to fill this
   Insatiable, all-consuming urge
   I need to get back to my work
   Talking to myself, this is absurd

But if I pick up the phone
   And type a quick "hru" text
   I'll just plant a seed
   We will see what it leads to next

Playing a dangerous game
   Cause if there is a reply
   Too weak to turn down anything
   Everything's on the table, I ain't gonna lie

My flesh has taken me over
  Now is a good time to pray
  To pull out some scriptures and read
  But I don't want to chase this feeling away

In this moment I am weak as water
  I want to feel this tingly sensation
  Y'all know what I'm talking about
  Urges that cause all sorts of anticipation

But they cause other thoughts too
  Thoughts of regret and walks of shame
  Especially after you've done the deed
  And reflect on your actions again

Text sitting here looking at me
  Should I do it, should I press send
  Why is this such a struggle for me
  Always this battle raging within

Don't be afraid of his reaction
  I know he will tell me he's coming
  Maybe it's my reaction that scares me
  Maybe what I'm becoming keeps me running

Lord, what should I do
  Uh oh, I asked You, now I know I'm done
  Feeling starting to dissipate
  Not completely gone, but some

Why did I call on the Lord?
  Now feeling a whole 'nother feeling
  Guilt and shame, this flesh I can't tame

All these emotions have got me reeling

Backspacing the letters, I typed
    Distraction defeated for today
    Tomorrow, if it should return
    How will I react? I don't know. Can't say.

Mark 4:14-20

Don't Want to Give Up on Love

In spite of the flaws in me I see
    Despite the hate, you have for me
    I want to cling to love

For the hate you give leaves no place
    For forgiveness, mercy, or saving grace
    Only pain and vengeance can fill hate's space
    It should not hurt to love

Hate plants its ever-growing seed
    Ignorance, the flower it continuously breeds
    Sometimes I think it fills my needs
    It masquerades as a form of love

But Love does not truth defy
    Nor my suffering will it deny
    I don't want to give up on love
    Ephesians 4:2

Embrace Who You Are

Come, my Two Heartbeats!
   Get comfortable; take a seat
   Let me tell you a wondrous tale
   Of the many times, I had to fail

For you see me as I am now, my dears
   Not as I was then, back through the years
   Afraid of the adventures that lay before me
   But eager to explore what I thought I could be

If you only knew the blunders I made
   The roads I traveled, though signs forbade
   I would tell you of love gained only to be lost
   I'd travel them again though they came with a cost

See the lines on my face and gray of my hair
   Reminders of the memories I created there
   All of me molded and shaped by my travels
   Tossed and torn, yet refusing to unravel

Friendships and joy I gained along the way
   Still a part of our lives 'til this very day
   Sisterhoods formed, not born of a mother
   Blue and gold ties that bind us one to the other

Bonds undeniable forged by turbulent winds
   Storms and fires that shaped me within
   All of my past sculpting the clay
   That would make me the person I am today

Would not change any good, bad or sad times
   It was all for my good, to shape my heart and my mind
   I want you to know that all that I am
   Good, bad, and ugly is part of my plan

There's no way you can grow if you do not know
   All sides of who you really are; let them show
   You will be tempted and hated, even berated
   At times you'll feel loved, celebrated, elated

As I look into your big brown eyes, I can see
   My hopes and my dreams staring back at me
   I am assured that your roads will lead you far
   And carry you to the fullness of who you are
   Romans 8:28; Psalm 37:25

Enough

What does it mean to be enough
  To have enough, to give enough
  Y'all life is tough

Sometimes feel like I've done enough
  Heard enough, said enough
  Boy, times get rough

Days when I have had enough
  Seen enough, prayed enough
  Feel like giving up

Screaming enough is enough
  I'm enough, you're enough
  Life, I'm calling your bluff

Fantasy

I drunk from loves cup
  Now I'm wondering, what's up
  Fantasy out working reality,
  Man, that's a tragedy

Remember my thoughts of him
  How he'd come over on a whim
  Sweep me off my feet
  Have me clinging on to sheets

Remember the dreams I had
  Those nights in bed that drove me mad
  Couldn't get to him, feeling sad
  A good girl, wanting to be bad

What happened to all of that
  How do we flip, and get that back
  Turn on an eighties love track
  Him on the phone talking smack

I remember when I heard him say
  There was this game he wanted to play
  Distance kept us from getting our way
  But in this present time today, delay, delay, delay, delay.

Relying on old memories
   Of how he'd bring me to my knees
   Have me gently saying "please"
   Getting heated thinking about days like these

Fantasies, why do they out last
   Always dressing up the past
   Sure, my life has been a blast
   But, reality needs to get up off its ass

How do I get her back to the reaction
   That drove our satisfaction
   I know she's in there relaxing
   But, your girl could really use some passion

Favor

Thank you for favor
   That protects me from me
   Not allowing me to become
   What I'm not supposed to be

Not filled with envy
   And always longing for things
   Never intended to bestow joy
   Or the stature I think it would bring

Plucked from me
   A jealous eye wanting another's life
   Angry with them about their success
   Never knowing or caring about their strife

Removing from me
   The want and the greed
   That promises everything
   That would to emptiness lead

Thank you for giving me
   No pleasure to destroy
   But a desire to grow and build up
   Therein lies all my joy

No futile thoughts
   Meant to steal and kill
   Self-destruction, it's useless path
   Many destinies unfulfilled

Thank you for the wisdom in knowing
   It's not the favor of things
   But the favor of not wanting
   My Lord, the peace and freedom that brings

For those who seek favor
   As opportunity and election
   I thank you for the realization
   That favor wraps me in your protection

Psalm 30:5

Flawed

Judge me because I'm flawed, of course you do
   But, while you are judging me someone is judging you
   As humans we are all defective beings who are weak
   Instead of appraising others, self-assessment we should seek

Adjudicating my own character would seem a better exercise
   To re-examine my character flaws that are leading to my demise
   To shift my paradigm, my view about how I contend with another
   Undoubtedly begins with a thorough self-introspection, that could be a
spirit crusher

Or perhaps, it will renew in my spirit this sincere look at who I truly am
   Lord knows I've spent enough time evaluating others, failing them on
every exam
   I will take myself to task and look back from past to my present
   Unwrap the things that I've done, those that were good, and those less
pleasant

I will compare myself to no one, for I know I will be ashamed
   Just thinking about this exercise makes me want to never judge another
again
   So, what?! My sins are not theirs, but my sins are sins all the same
   While man may judge me lightly, I'm not playing by man's rules in life's
game

Judge not, that ye be not judged for the rules that you set, if they're cruel
   Will be used against you in such a time that you think you have the world
fooled
   If you sincerely wish to help your fellow man and not hinder his path
   Pray for him and speak words of truth to his face, do not behind his back
judge him and then laugh

Your judgments are not very useful, though harsh tones may at times be
needed
   If you walk in the light of your purpose, you will be given instruction;
heed it
   Instruction not given in love, but to mock, or deflect, or to blame
   Is a denial that you, too are flawed, and you are playing a dangerous game

Souls are on the line; life is the cost of the words and deeds we do
   We must learn to love one another even as we are going through
   When we know better it is our impetus to do better and to show
   Though I am flawed I am willing, in my faith, to learn and to grow

Matthew 7:1-5

Forgive and Forget

Why must I forgive and forget
   The abuses of my offender
   The answer lies not in the forgetting
   But in how I choose to remember

Why should I forgive the transgressions of those
   Who sought to render me helpless
   Forgetting the pain and hurt inflicted
   Gives brand new meaning to selfless

To forgive your dishonesty
   To forgive your inadequacy
   To forgive total disloyalty
   To forgive you, I must examine me

To forget all the lies that were told
   To forget how you vexed my soul
   To forget how you did this, so bold
   To forget allows me to break your hold

To forgive sins born out of ignorance
   Does not happen overnight, you see
   To forget has required wisdom and time
   And I have done so unwittingly

While I forgave a long time ago
    So that I would not be bitter and lonely
    Forgetting the pain and the shame of your hurt
    Is something that time could heal, only

But to say I forgot is a misnomer
    It's better for me to reframe
    It is how I choose to remember
    And how I grew in spite of the pain

I understood your purpose in my story
    Was to teach me a painful lesson
    Sure, I didn't want to learn at the time
    But over the years, it has become mine or someone else's blessing

Taken in totality
    Whether loss or victory
    Your time was meant to be
    To plant a seed in me

So, I forgive you as the actor
    Playing out your role
    I remember how I resented you
    For the joy I thought you stole

I forgive you the pain inflicted
    I thought without reason
    I remember now that you were a part
    Of my growing season

I forgive these days
    Not because it's easy to forget
    But because I choose to remember the lessons

Not live life with bitterness and regret

Ephesians 4:32

For My Good & His Glory

Struggles on my road
 Cursed everyone, right or wrong
 Clueless to the fact
 They were for my good all along

Laughs behind my back
 Some blatantly in my face
 Tears I cried not knowing
 The turmoil is guiding me "some" place

Questioning my looks
 Sometimes looks sent my way
 Disgusted with my failures
 Designed to prep me for "some" day

Barely making payments
 Letters on the table saying overdue
 Feels like I'm wasting space
 Yet, gray skies giving way to blue

Please hold on a little longer
 Keep striving toward your goal
 Tribulations not here to rip you apart
 On the contrary, they make you whole

As I read over the pages
     Found within my life's story
     I thank Him for my troubles
     Meant for my good, and for His glory

1 Corinthians 15:55-58

Fruit of Your Labor

The fruit of your labor
  Has gained God's mercy, His favor
  Though some may disregard what we all know is true
  The glory of the hand of God hidden in plain view

Your determination and prayers
  Have lifted your seed, your heirs
  From horrors unseen, unawares

For in bonds and filth you came to shore
  But, encrusted in the shame of bondage, no more
  Your heritage has built many a door
  A solid foundation, not a floor
  To raise your legacy that you bore

For enslaved did not equate
  To an incapable or incompetent fate
  An unknown language and land you did take
  And refuse to let it break
  The spirit of a people, for generations' sake

The wonder and the glory
  That would become your improbable story
  Rest in peace and power and do not worry

Your children are relearning that they are worthy

From enslavement to pounding pavement
  To hosting a penthouse engagement
  From tobacco fields to Beverly Hills
  From believing, I won't to knowing I will
  The overflowing gratitude that my heart feels
  Can never be paid with any paper bill

This is the unimaginable legacy you left for me
  One that you never got to see come to be
  Through your toils, and tears, and misery
  I owe you the respect, honor, and dignity
  Of an impossible legacy that was never 'supposed to be'

But whether through fashion or through rhyme
  We became the fascination of our time
  Still learning to lift as we climb
  So as not to leave anyone behind

Sculpting, painting, and building a nation
  We became the envy of generations
  Praising God for deliverance and salvation
  Still awaiting the ultimate emancipation

We are the fruit of the labor of the slave
  Find peace and rest beyond the grave
  God heard your plea, and He did save
  The rest of the way is now ours to pave

Psalm 118; Matthew 7:16-17

Getting Over You

Laughable, impossible
    Won't even bother to try
    Deeply buried within my conscience
    Innumerable ways to say goodbye

Desire always at the surface
    Wanting to come out again
    To experience the life of lovers
    But that was not in our plan

Demented fate or twisted time
    Never on our side
    Forgetting you, not in the cards,
    Thoughts tormenting wounded pride

Put one foot in front of the other
    Though life, at times, lacked clarity
    Life can't be a useless wasteland
    Me floating through it, no gravity

Plant my feet in bittersweet moments
    Of a love not meant to take root
    Grow in a sincere faith and hope
    That allows my heart time to reboot

In time the rays of love,
Raindrops of mercy will reveal
A tree rooted in favor and grace
Producing a heart that over time will heal

Giving Up

I couldn't give up on me
   Cause that would've meant giving up on you
   And without you in my life
   What on Earth would I be purposed to do

Giving up when I lost my mother
   Would've eased so much of my pain
   But the fine tuning and heavy-lifting I'd gone through
   All the work on me wasted - in vain

Lessons I learned as a child
   Some repeated as an adult, unlearned
   Giving up would've been such a waste
   No yield on my investments returned

Imperative for me that patience and I
   Would finally learn to co-exist
   Had I not kept pushing through life's hard times
   A life of love and laughter with you I'd miss

Giving up and leaving it all behind
   Not a choice I ever wanted to choose
   But life gets tricky and confusing at times
   Making us feel we've nothing to lose

I'm never giving up on you or us
  I am never giving up on me
  Trials, tribulations, come what may
  I choose to live as one who is free

Go

Should I go slow
 Just dip my toe
 Man, I don't know

Should I listen to shouts
 In my mind crying out
 Full of fear, laced with doubt

Or do I dare trust
 That thing inside of us
 Imploring me, I must

Gotta take a leap of faith
 Always been my saving Grace
 Only way I know to run my race

My biggest fear
 That they won't hear
 Father, please hold them near

Don't want to add stress
 But to their burdens, give less
 If they would to You, all confess

Got my marching orders
   Won't live life as a hoarder
   Keeping His goodness within my borders

Time to share what I know
   This is not for show, can't be slow
   Ready or not, let's GO!

Colossians 3:2-17

Go Get Your Children

Where are your babies at this darkest hour?
    Somewhere withering away as an untended flower.
    Better question maybe why did you let them go?
    Been warned about allowing them to go to and fro.

Where is our future that we allow the world to devour?
    Not yet prepared because we armed them with no power.
    Sent to fight a battle with video games as their weapon.
    Doomed to lose the war if we don't soon go and get them.

Lack of discipline and desire will lead to sure defeat.
    Never taught structure in the home, just tricks of chaos in the street.
    Go get your children before it is too late
    To turn back from the cruelty of a predictable, fatal fate.

Go get your children and tell them you've been wrong
    Sitting on your behind and wasting time for much too long
    Gotta get your children before we run outta time
    No way I'd ever let this world have a child of mine

Don't you love your children? Then show them you know how.
    It's okay you've made mistakes along the way, do better now.
    Go get your children! I know you love them just need insight
    To pull you from the complacency and help you get this right.

Let's go get our children, no lost cause under our care.
Might be a winding road to find them no turning round 'til we get there.
And when we get our children, hold them tight in your arm.
Let them feel your protection so they will know they are safe from harm.

Ephesians 6:4; Proverbs 22:6

Handle with Care

Vulnerability, self-exposure.
   What if I lose my composure?

Sharing intimate parts of myself.
   My life sitting on another's shelf.

My life always hidden, quite mundane.
   Stepping into the spotlight, man this feels insane.

Am I really doing this at this point in my existence?
   Writing my innermost thoughts, probably overdue, isn't it?

My thoughts and my heart laid bare
   If only I could label this, "Handle with Care"

Not turning back now as I obey God's lead.
   Hope it serves its purpose and blesses each one as they read.

1 Samuel 15:22

Heart's Breaking

Heartache
  Makes for heart break
  Not much more one can take
  When missing the soul's mate

The memories
  They never leave
  Refuse to let the heart grieve
  Deny the mind merciful reprieve

Pretending, trying
  Eyes that won't cease crying
  A mind, constantly denying
  Wasting time, caught up in lying

Heart in danger
  Feeling tinges of anger
  Going through life with a stranger
  Bonded together, but no love to anchor

Feeling lonely
  Without your one, your only
  Not a way to end in glory
  No happy ending to love's story

Psalm 34:18

Help Me Grow

You say you do not understand why I behave as I do
   A word of consolation, you were never supposed to

My life was created for me to live as I see fit
   Not to be judged by the masses, dissected bit by bit

The whispers that are never far behind the scars left on my back
   Created from the sharpness of invisible knives my friends pack

But friendship is supposedly different, I thought, a unique creature
   It bears kindness and love, and trust, the most coveted feature

Words of encouragement would be nice coming from a friend or two
   They often come far and few, linked to a price that is always due

If my best interest is truly what a friend has at the center of their heart
   Shouldn't they grant me a little grace and mercy, let patience play its part?

I am a human being, constantly being made, constantly taking shape
   How wonderful it would be if throughout life I made no mistakes

Is that how friends live their lives, perfectly without a smear or blot
   Seems too much time rebuking others has become their predictable lot

Still, I take loving advice and pack it in the corners of my mind
   It will be there when I need it if there should ever come a time

My friends are precious to me, and I try to keep them in the know
   I love sharing my life with them who don't hinder but help me grow.

1 Thessalonians 5:11; Matthew 12:33

Here I come

Quiet and sweet
   Even-tempered and meek
   Obedient as a child
   While meanwhile

A surging tide
   Brewing deep inside
   Unleashing a voice
   Giving me little choice

Words taking shape
   From my brain, they'd escape
   Landing on the page
   What's next, the stage

Blowing my mind
   But I'll know in due time
   Be obedient, gain refinement
   Show you know your assignment

Deuteronomy 5:33

History Erased...Heritage Forsaken

When was good enough ever great
    Surely, this isn't up for debate

Striving to the bottom to be mediocre
    Is this what they hoped and prayed for?

Our hidden figures obscured without reason
    Not allowed to shine within their season

We must reveal each one and bring into view
    Their work to be acclaimed; give credit where due

We must shine on them and tell their story
    Not just live in the remnant of their glory

I never thought myself a harvesting man, granted
    'Til I realized I am reaping what others planted

To replenish the harvest for next season's crops
    We must get busy; this is no time to rest; to stop

My job may be to plant, not shine the sun or water the ground
    The one who controls nature will make sure my seeds are found

The seeds will get what they need to help their roots to grow
My job is not to question, my work is just to stand and show

For our children's sake we must take the map we have been shown
And carry on the legacy of those who are the lesser known

Learn the history of us, and just like in them, it will awaken
A desire to ensure your children's heritage is not forsaken

1 John 4:4

How Much Does Free Speech Cost

Is speech free, or does it come at a cost?
  Like a livelihood or a life lost.
  Is speech free? What if I take a knee, publicly?
  But you disagree with me? Will you let me be?

Pray tell, what amount will it cost my bank account?
  If I disagree with those in opposition, if they don't like my disposition?
  Well, can't be too concerned. I'm on a mission.

Is speech only free in certain spaces?
  To certain races?
  Only if I grin in certain faces?

Maybe I should hold back, no time to talk smack.

Free speech seems like an oxymoron.
  Only meant for some.
  Relied upon in days long gone.

Free speech has come with unspeakable cost,
  For some heartbreak and loss,
  Others' bank accounts and businesses tossed,
  Reputations in taters and buried beneath the moss.

Free speech is considered indispensable.
   Yet, used for the indefensible
   To create suffering that is incomprehensible

Human taxation upon those in a nation who can ill afford placation

The invaluable speech that we speak must be spoken.
   If those words can prevent minds, bodies, and souls from being broken.
   No one wants to be used as a token.
   The words in my heart, I refuse to choke on.

Will I continue to be free, or will my words sting?
   Cost me everything?
   On freedom's song I will stand and sing.
   Take my chances, the cost of silence is too much. Let freedom ring.

Romans 13:7-8

Hypocrisy

Freely giving advice to others
  While living with a forbidden lover
  What hypocrisy is this

Prescribing to others how to live
  Seemingly ignoring counsel, you often give
  Your hypocrisy dismissed

Living life in a wanton lane
  Nothing there for you to gain
  Hypocrisy brings about loss

Love of money and worldly power
  Will decency and conviction devour
  Hypocrisy - too high your cost

Galatians 6:3; Luke 6:46

Image

Everyone thinking you're the best
    You're a mess

Busy putting on your lovely mask
    Failing tasks

Presenting as always being picture perfect
    Hope it's worth it

Hiding deep cuts and wounds from internal wars
    We see the scars

From the podium you think you're always schooling
    You're not fooling

Refusing to recognize your many flaws
    No valid cause

Destroying lives you promised to protect
    What'd you expect

Prosperity can't be found in an image built behind disguise
    We see the lies

Thought you played everyone around and they'd do your will
  Not the deal

Truth revealed to all adoring fans and perfect image stained
  Reminding me of Cain

Psalm 55:21; Proverbs 26:23-25

I'm Me

I may not be the loveliest, most definitely not the worldliest,
   Do I need to be, I'm glad that I am me

I may not be the smartest, I may not work the hardest,
   Why judge me for being me

I'm not adorned in someone else's name, not seeking someone else's fame,
   Yet it seems to bother you that I am me

I love the freedom of who I am, when I choose to be my number one fan,
   I love me some me

Focus on you like you focus on me, learn to love self and God completely!
   Am I envious of you? Why should I be? I'm me!

Psalm 139:14

Imperfect Me

An imperfect world
　For an imperfect girl
　An imperfect spirit such as me

Learning to exist
　Between sadness and bliss
　Undulating, trying to discover where I'm supposed to be

Imperfect stance
　By circumstance
　Following all the days of my life

Why do they stare?
　Learn not to care
　The better part of me must suffice

Imperfect skin
　I'm living in
　Or so I hear them whisper as I walk by

The way I speak
　Makes me a geek
　Seems others not happy unless they make me cry

Twisted logic
    Yeah, I got it
    Must adjust quickly to stay in the game

Cruelty taught?
    Surely not
    If parents knew, wouldn't they be ashamed?

Dwell on my imperfection
    Under constant scrutiny, inspection
    Who needs their acceptance anyway?

Heavy burden
    But I'm learning
    It doesn't matter the negative words they say

Confidence building
    I'm not yielding
    Any of my power 'cause I have a plan

Time on my side
    Learning to let things slide
    As I learn to love the imperfect me that I am

2 Peter 3:18; Philippians 3:12-14

In Love with Love

We do this dance together
  Yes, always with each other
  Watching, waiting for the other to break

And though I say I love you
  Place no one else in this world above you
  I push you to the limit never knowing how much you'll take

I question our forever
  Thinking I should know you better
  I should cherish every moment that we share

But sometimes when I feel lonely
  Not feeling like your one, your only
  Only feeling my heart and soul exposed, stripped bare

In love with love, I want to go
  In love with love, I never know
  In love with love, I fall fast and slow
  In love with love, 'til I love no more

Why do I dance this solemn dance
  Take this turbulent, unpredictable chance
  Finding happiness in arms not meant for me

Because I need to feel the warmth
    Feel the strength of a lover's arms
    Wrapped around me, taking me where I long to be

In love with love, I want to go
    In love with love, I never know
    In love with love, I fall fast and slow
    In love with love, 'til I love no more

What am I supposed to do
    Do I keep on loving you
    When you can't love me like I need you to
    Do I keep hiding my tears
    As they keep rolling, the years
    Since I stood before you and promised, I do

In love with love, I want to go
    In love with love, I never know
    In love with love, I fall fast and slow
    In love with love, 'til I love no more

1 Corinthians 13:1-8, 13

Just Like You

You think that I am strong
   I'm as vulnerable as any other
   Miss the days of picking up the phone
   Crying and complaining to my mother

To hear her voice and laughter
   Didn't matter time of day
   She would always my calls answer
   My doubts and fears she would allay

My pains, heartaches, and criticisms
   Disappointments and failures, all real
   She'd remind me I am not supernatural
   I am a human with the capacity to feel

Capable of reaching the highest heights
   But tumbling to the lowest low
   I could choose to wallow in despair
   Or shake off another blow

For my God knows my deepest thoughts
   He comes to see about you and me
   Sends His angels if rescue is needed
   He waits for us patiently, you see

Just like you, He wants me to call on Him
 When things get out of hand
 Just like you, life gets hard sometimes
 I feel I can't meet all of its demands

Just like you, I hope for love to abide
 And for my family to stay safe from harm
 Just like you, I make mistakes and stumble
 There is no need for alarm

In the midst of our troubles
 There is one thing I am assured of
 Just like you, I want protection
 So, I set my sight on things above
 How about you? What do you do?

Jeremiah 17:7-8

Just Mary

Mary, tough, hard-headed
   Impossible to understand.
   That is, until you see her
   Through the blood of the lamb.

Stubborn in her ways
   Tough in her love and stance.
   Thought to be mean-spirited
   If you read her at first glance.

By His mercy, grace, and favor
   He gave her a brand-new manner of speech.
   He graced her with a language to use
   So, others she could teach.

He changed the way she slumbered.
   He purposed the way she moves.
   The limp with which she walks
   Just a distraction that He used.

Who is this, Mary,
   That the Lamb protects each day?
   No hair on her head can be touched
   Unless He takes His protection away.

She is a powerful force to be reckoned
  Yet, she is no saint or martyr.
  She merely accepts her worldly place.
  She is the Almighty's daughter.

Excelling in this life
  But, she still remains a humble stranger.
  She moves within her purpose
  Not fearful of any unseen danger.

She knows to whom she belongs.
  The only One she chooses to please.
  By being just Mary, she finds there is no joy
  To bend or break just to appease.

Just Mary, such a wonderful freedom
  Of spirit to live within her space.
  To love who she was created to be
  And allow others the same grace.
  Galatians 4:7

Know Your Place

Often it has been said that a woman should know her place
   When to speak, how to dress, how to accept an embrace

All the definitions and the roles that are unfurled
   Piled at her feet and given to her by this world

After all the woman is the weaker vessel, the second link in the chain
   Created for the purpose of man, or at least, so some explain

She is to be there when needed and keep quiet when told
   To speak her mind and vote her choice? Does she dare be so bold?

Don't fret, there are times when being a woman can come in handy
   To hold her man down, back him up, link arms and be his eye-candy

Ladies, know your place, I am not in disagreement all
   I am sure that I know mine, I have accepted my call

Whether writing or orating I hope that I am clear
   That my place and my space go far beyond this hemisphere

Not defined by worldly attributes given to me by a man
   Gifted to me be my Creator when He informed me of His plan

My walk is not your walk and my femininity while peculiar
    Maybe intimidating to some, to some even obscure

I need no branding clothes or jewels to make my place known
    Not every queen that walks this Earth must sit upon a throne

My place is one of favor, love, mercy, and saving grace
    Given by my Father and by you, cannot be erased

My place is one not limited by doors you may try to close
    Attempting to look down at me, daring to thumb your nose

My place is one that has a ceiling not made of impenetrable glass
    But made of a certain fabric in my veins that's built to surpass

My place is one I am certain that is not limited by wages that live on floors,
    Now that I know my place, tell me, do you know yours?

Jeremiah 29:11

Knowing Love

I knew of you in my youth
   Blindly and innocently
   Impatiently awaiting
   The day when you'd finally know me

Thought the time had come
   Thought we'd made a connection
   Daydreaming about the one
   Who was the object of my affection

Only teenagers then
   What did we know of you
   Thought you only tender and kind
   Not realizing you show cruelty too

He noticed me and I him
   "Meet me for a kiss", I remember he said
   I agreed wanting to experience him
   But if Daddy finds out, we're both dead

Nervous all that fateful day
   Waiting for the bell to ring
   My teacher looking right at me
   Surely he doesn't know anything

What if he knows our plan
   To meet behind the school
   My reputation tarnished
   I will look like the biggest fool

So afraid I was by the time
   That we were supposed to meet
   I left him abandoned
   Waiting for me and my cold feet

He mistook my fear for rejection
   My hopes to know you dashed
   He graduated soon after
   But surely this is a mere detour on our path

Now home from basic training
   I saw him at a store
   'Go tell him you fool'
   This is the perfect chance to explore

See if he still feels the same
   Or if his heart's moved on
   Explain that you were just afraid
   Tell him that you were wrong

Foolish is pride when it appears
   And makes us swallow words
   I'd never see him after that day
   My apology would go unheard

This boy, my very first crush

Would in a car crash die
I heard the news in front of others
I couldn't let the tears escape my eye

So, love, I didn't meet you
    Not back then when you were in my grasp
    But since then I have feared you
    Yet, my heart you continuously harass

Afraid to truly know you
    Or believe what others think
    Beauty and purity, your calling card
    But I've seen you break hearts on the brink

I know your ways too well
    In my youth, a victim of what you can do
    But I'll protect myself from your volatile ways
    Don't believe me? Watch. I will show you.

1 Corinthians 13:1-2

Ladies It Has Always Been Our Time

When will it be my time to shine?
   There goes that constant whine.
   We've always known how to grind.

So, I say without reservation
   With no hesitation
   Lacking any trepidation,
   With some indignation
   That should have never been the question

It has always been our time
   Dust off the cobwebs in your mind
   The fallacies that allow you to bind
   The talent the world needs you to find
   And leave childish and foolish thoughts behind
   To the top of the mountain, we must climb
   RIGHT NOW, is OUR TIME TO Shine
   For we were created by the design of the Divine
   To take our place in line, and age as a fine wine

Recalibrate ladies and take your place
   For since your birth, the day you did grace
   The world with the beauty of your face
   We seemed to forget how to run this race

Allowing others to interpret our space
Dressing us in skimpy satin and lace
Like our minds should be erased
For the use of our bodies, for goodness sake

You may choose to disagree
  That's alright. This is my decree
  I can be wise and lovely
  I don't have to sacrifice one for the other. Really?
  To satisfy someone's fantasy of me
  And line their pockets lucratively
  Because He who created me
  Told me MY TIME was ALWAYS, not lately
  Use your talents, my beloved, wisely
  And you, too, will see
  When she asks, "Mama when will my time be?"
  You can say unwaveringly
  "You were born to use your talents freely,
  Today, tomorrow, go let the world see
  For you are, Little Lady, the best of me"

Genesis 2:18-22

Lashes and Lips

You think the cleavage and the hips
   Making him want to take a dip

Just got to my place
   Can't get past my face

The lashes and lips
   Got his mind doing flips

Noticing the hazel of my eyes
   Got my man hypnotized

Slow down, boy, be a gent
   I'm a marathon not a sprint

Batting my eyes and being coy
   Bringing him so much joy

Fire engine red on these lips
   While my drink I slowly sip

Gets him every time
   These ain't even mine

End of our time drawing nigh
   Still got my baby flying high

Sitting at the table he grabs my chair
   Now face to face, in each other's eyes we stare

He smiles at me knowingly
   Awaiting my approval to let it be

The kissing game, lame so they say
   Obviously they don't know how to play

Sensations impossible to explain
   Activating every pleasure center in my brain

Now off to bed to dream of me and my king
   Thanks lashes and lips for the joy you bring

Song of Solomon 4:1-3

Lessons

Many of my blessings
  Have come from life's lessons

Hard as they were to take
  Many born of my foolish mistakes

Daydreaming, wasting time
  Longing for something not yet mine

Patience, my most challenging class
  Try as I might, can't seem to pass

Keep taking tests already seen
  Not learning information I'm supposed to glean

These exams can't afford to fail
  But, boy, some of them whipping my tail

Told me to study to show myself approved
  I'm so hard-headed, an intelligent fool

Copying others, looking for life's cheat codes
  Knowing better, making lengthy my road

Multiple choice got too many choices
    Open book, my soul rejoices

Got me reading; what is this
    Answers dating back to Genesis

Numbers and Psalms make Revelations
    Got me engaged; part of the conversation

This is wild; I had no idea
    You teaching me about You, always in here

All the hard lessons I've had to learn, not in vain
    Blessing me to do Your will from my predestined lane

2 Timothy 2:15

Let Him In

So often we question
  Why won't he rescue us
  Everything falling apart
  Don't see him, why should we trust

I offer you this thought
  He's knocking, let Him in
  What, you don't hear Him
  Be still, listen again

I know your mother believed
  I know you understand that part
  He wants you to believe
  With your mind and your whole heart

Can't depend on another's faith
  To rescue you from the abyss
  Close out the other noises
  Listen for the voice, uniquely His

You'll know it when you hear it
  You've probably shut it out before
  He asked you to give up some things
  This time don't ignore

He only speaks the truth
    He only expects actions that are pure
    If you can't discern His voice from others
    If you are still unsure

Ask Him to reveal himself to you
    Search the words He left behind
    Instructions there abound
    Within the pages Him you will find

He wants you to feel His presence
    You feel you can't find Him anywhere
    Once you learn to hear His voice
    He'll tell you He's always been right there

Carrying you over ditches
    You didn't even see
    Protecting you from thunderbolts
    Aimed to strike their targets precisely

Shielding you from shadows
    Only meant to cause you fear
    Protecting you from unseen dangers
    Though you never acknowledged He was near

Your only awareness came
    When your wants and desires were not fulfilled
    Did you ever ask Him once
    Or even care if that was His will

Just maybe that thing you wanted
    Or that situation that caused you pain
    Was unpleasant and seemed unbearable

But it was ultimately for your gain

As we motion through everyday life
    With this stubborn unwillingness to bend
    Maybe take some time to seek His face
    Learn His ways and let Him in

Don't judge Him by man's standards
    What a foolish mistake to make
    We want from God a one-way relationship
    But it is one of give and take

No need to feel as though
    You walk through your journey alone
    We look for Him in others' houses
    Try inviting Him into your own

Psalm 34:17

Let Me

Those overwhelming feelings that you've tried to hide
  You know, the ones you've drug around, buried deep inside

The pain that no one sees, and no one can feel but you
  Let me help you ease the load. Please allow me to.

I know I act indifferent, and it seems I could care less
  So consumed with my problems and my own happiness

But I have room to carry the distresses of another
  Especially for those who I call my sister or my brother

If I wake tomorrow and I find that you are gone
  You went off and left me here because you faced your hurt alone

My heart would forever be fractured and my mind forever haunted
  Knowing and agonizing that I could not give you the support that you
wanted

For you see if you leave here and don't say good-bye or tell me why
  Without giving me a chance to be there, then a part of me would die

Was I not a friend at all that you didn't think that you could call
  When life was at its lowest point and was causing you to fall

Let my hand be there for the taking, I have the strength I know it
   How devastating for all of us if I never got the chance to show it

That's all I want to say. I needed to be sure you knew the plan
   When you're lost and no one else will, take this plan in your hand

There's nothing we can't face together and yes, I can sacrifice
   Nothing is worth giving you up, together we will fight to save your life.

Proverbs 17:17; Romans 12:9-10

Love of Many Mothers

I have been blessed with the love of many mothers
    Wrapped in the comfort of their prayer-filled covers
    They kept me safe and protected from harm

While I coveted the love of a nameless man
    Who never came and met the expectations that no man can
    The glow of their love kept my cold heart warm

Their joy, their chatter, their love, and laughter
    A true and pure, happily ever after
    No love more powerful than that of my other mother's, who

Adopted me into their family as one of their own
    For when the loving embrace of my mama was gone
    They stood beside me so that I would not be alone
    Out of my sorrow, the love from my mothers pulled me through
    Proverbs 31:25-31

Love of My Life

Love of my life, I've a confession
  No longer able to conceal my affection
  My heart rejecting my protection
  No need to speak, just listen

I've loved you all my life
  At least as long as I can remember
  My soul beckoning to yours to save me
  Your body tempting mine to surrender

Lost in the promise of paradise
  Your kisses so sweet, so tender
  Unaware of the true sacrifice
  In love's game, a rookie, a beginner

Oblivious to the ache love can cause
  Defiant of its critics' caution
  Only know that I need you near me
  Your sweet remedy, I need it often

Such mystery shrouds my emotions
  Others questioning if this love is real
  My fate twisted in the palm of your hands
  No one can comprehend how it is that I feel

Not even I know the depths of my adoration
    This love my heart holds for you
    This tangible emotional connection
    Making me do things I never imagined I'd do

The control-freak lost all control
    The good girl gone terribly bad
    What am I to do now that I'm tainted
    All of this conflict driving me mad

This love has such a powerful pull
    A hold that is stronger than my will
    Try and try as I might to runaway
    It chips away at the distance I build

Not running anymore, giving up
    Forgot why I was running at all
    For once in my life, I want to let go
    Please catch me when in your arms, I fall

Love - Take One

It's not that I don't love you anymore
　　Better stated, I don't love you as before
　　Love something different for us, let's explore

In the beginning fun times and romance filled our past
　　Neither of us at the time thought it meant to last

Having a friend, experiencing something new
　　Back then, it felt like the right thing to do

Decided that marriage was the next logical step
　　Couldn't foresee the future trials, the arguments on rep

Selfish nature revealed as we peeled back layers
　　Me ready to leave, to be traded on waivers

Raising children adding flavor to the daunting task
　　Marriage already a challenge, should anyone ask

Learning habits that are created and bound to annoy
　　Distracting from building relationship, tenderness, and joy

Navigating a life shared selflessly with another
　　Forsaking my wants for the needs of the other

Romance and good times giving way to practicality
    Fantasy and daydreaming move out the way for reality

Should've known front the start
    Destined to grow further apart
    Not of the same mind, following the foolish heart

Or was it the flesh that led to this dance
    Two lonely people finding comfort in their circumstance

As life has passed by, the love has changed
    Probably predictable, to some not that strange

When it comes to achievement, same dreams, different plans
    One satisfied in the moment, the other searching for where to land

Secured by trial and error, true love will stand
    The kind that blossoms when you learn your man

Especially those things I didn't understand
    Straining my patience, my time he demands

But me always present, that's a fact
    No matter what, I got his back

Gets tricky when he doesn't have mine
    That's when this love may not stand the test of time

Growing weary of the constant fight
    Having long talks with the Lord at night

Other options on my mind
    Should I move forward or stay behind

How did I get here…the hands of time

Writing this tale of a romance unravel
   Is a lesson in carefully choosing the road you travel

Especially if the road takes you to a place
   You must stay for a while and try to make your space

The home you buy or one you lease
   Should bring you comfort, hold your peace

Love comes in many forms and takes many shapes
   But that of a lover should not your spirit break

Not one to give relationship advice (but seek ye first)
   Take this cautionary tale for what it's worth

M & P, On a Date

P: Look at her act as cool as a cucumber
   I know better, last night she couldn't slumber

It's been years since we've been here, pretending like fire is ice
   Tonight's gonna bring out some spice

You can hear her heartbeat, feel it race
   Watch her chest rise and fall, can't even keep pace
   You know why, she just seen his face

M: Walk away now, before he sees
   Look away quick, don't be a tease

Flashing smiles, nervous laughter
   Who does he think he's fooling; I know what he's after

P: Wish she'd pay you some attention.
   I'm the game one, not the tame one
   I like to have fun. Oh, didn't I mention.
   It's time for the fun to begin.

Come sit down, turn around
   Come to me, let me see

It's been a while, damn that smile
   Those deep dimples, my mind went simple

Concentrate, what's on the menu
   No, not him. What's that? He missed you.

Speak those lies, touching thighs
   How'd we get so close? Shoot! There she goes.

M: Pulling back. Goes into attack
   P: Asking who he's with, ain't that a bitch?
   Now he's defensive, we're dismissive

My hard work slipping because she tripping.
   Dressed to make him beg. This dress, these legs.
   I'm taking over like a bulldozer
   Tonight, is mine cause this boy is fine

Did she just call him lazy?! Girl, you actin' crazy!

I didn't mean it, Baby. Look at me. Maybe
   We should start at the good part
   When you stared in my eyes, caught me by surprise
   Let's both say sorry get back to our party
   I didn't mean what I said, drink gone to my head.

Life's been treating you well, cause you fine as hell.
   What's come over me? Let's wait and see.
   You know what, call me Penny. You're a VIP.
   For you it seems normal, Mary seems much too formal.

If all ends right, by the end of the night
   By the time we are through, call me whatever you want to

M: I don't know what's in this cup. It's been nice catching up
    I don't mean to be a jerk, but I must go, you know, to work.
    NO! No need to see me home. I will be fine on my own.
    I'm sure you're busy and need your rest, I wish you the best.
    Thanks for the food and the wine. I had a nice time.
    Seeing you brought back memories, of when you and I used to be…
    Well, listen to me chatter, none of that even matters
    Thanks for walking me to my car. Yes, I see that shining star.
    I'm sure it's the darkness of the night, my eyes don't shine that bright.
    Gosh, I feel feverish, maybe it's from the dish

P: No, fool, it's from the kiss, he's about to put on our lips.
    You better not flinch, one little inch.
    Because knowing you, this is all we get to do.
    I want to enjoy every moment before I go back to the convent

M: That was nice. He's a nice guy. It's been a while since I…
    Ok, well, good-bye. Maybe we can do this again. I'd like to try.

P: Man, I knew she'd blow it. Need to loosen up some.
    M: I hope that he shows it. Let's me know that he's the one.

Malignancy

Malignancy waiting
    Treatment, debating
    Options, too many
    Fears gathering, plenty

Hope, do I dare
    Or cling to my despair
    Emotions twisted
    Responses unpredicted

Outcomes unfair
    Angry, can't care
    Romance, never tasted
    Pain, unabated

Purpose, unknown
    Time, soon gone
    Chance, have I another
    Dream, why bother

Fight or flight
    Wrongs done, made right
    Armor on, stand my ground
    Feeling lost, now found

Battle on, don't plan to lose
   Sword in hand, time to choose
   Malignancy multiplying
   Not going out without trying

Psalm 30:2

Man Up

When you say, *Man up*
   What exactly do you mean?
   I want to get it right
   Come on, come clean

When you say, *Man Up*
   Is that a call to be
   All the exquisite things
   You were meant to be for me?

When you say, *Man up*
   It gets my full attention.
   Gets me fired up
   But sometimes leaves me wishing.

When you say, *Man up*
   What is your definition?
   For I want to see your strength of mind
   Of all your convictions.

When you say, *Man up*
   Is it only self-gratifying
   Fake flex, fake wealth
   Exactly who are you satisfying?

When you say, *Man up*
   Am I expecting too much from you
   To show up and show out
   As a royal prince is supposed to do?

Cause when I say, *Man up*
   I know exactly what I mean
   Be the King that allows you
   To be worthy of me, your queen

Ephesians 4:1-3

Messy, But Good

Tenth grade year, I heard a teacher foretell
  "Young lady, you're going straight to hell"
  Not a great way for her to try to sell
  A lost soul on a lesson on how to prevail

The message was messy, but she meant if for good
  Me not baptized into a church, but what of my personhood
  Sadly, my elder had me misunderstood
  She judged what she thought she knew, as others would

Early in life not prepared for life's test
  Opinionated about everything, thought I knew best
  Until I knew the judgment of others, I must confess
  I didn't realize that living upright looked like living in a mess

Same school, different year; for now, I am a senior
  Valedictorian of the class, yes, the sinner is a leader
  After graduation an encounter with a different teacher
  Would set the tone for my faith and make me a true believer

Off to college I wanted to go, twenty-five dollars to my name
  Forms completed, acceptance to the university came
  No money available to pay my way, I needed somebody to blame
  Feeling defeated and disgusted, I hung my head in shame

No college graduation day for me, or becoming what I thought I could be
    Dreams deferred and denied, maybe deservedly
    But my miracle, a teacher's tremendous generosity
    Taught me the meaning of living out true Christianity

She never spoke of God, or Christ, or faith, I swear it
    But she taught me instead of speaking faith, I should learn to wear it
    If Christ's love abides in me I should know how to share it
    In my deeds folks would see; but in words not walked, just spare it

At eighteen I did not know what I would grow up to be
    I did not know if one day I'd be poor or wealthy
    Or if I would be blessed one day with the ability
    To bless others as my teacher had unselfishly blessed me

To be a true light that shines on a hill
    Means living and working with good and pure will
    Being messy comes easy but it might be the wrong pill
    To prescribe to a world that's suffering from a deadly ill

Romans 5:8; Romans 8:39

Mirror, Mirror on the Wall: Time to Reflect

I hate looking in the mirror when it dares me to be
   Something great and remarkable when mediocrity is all I see
   I barely know who I am in this moment, or what is to become of me
   How will I ever come to know what I was meant to be?
   Does the answer lie in my past; is it locked in my ancestry?
   Is it locked away in my mind, buried in the deepest part of me?
   Is that why my ears refuse to listen, and my eyes find it impossible to see
   What others keep telling me is the better part of me?

When I look in the mirror, all these eyes of mine can see
   Is an ordinary person trying day-to-day just to be
   Not a failure, not a nuisance, not a body of hopeless misery
   Sometimes I want my reflection to disappear and come back as someone
else, you see
   For there are days that I feel not strong enough to weather this stormy sea
   But my reflection stares back as though it is daring me
   To be all that the ancestors, and my mother prayed I'd be
   It is that reflection that whispers gently "you already have the victory
   So, when you feel as though hope is lost and the world has needlessly
   Turned its back on you and reminded you of all it said you'd never be
   Return to your reflection for the TRUE you will always see
   Reminded here, in times of fear, that you are more than the conqueror

you were born to be
   Now, look again in the mirror, and tell me that you see the YOU, I see"

Romans 8:31-39

Meant To

I meant to love you better
   Swear I didn't know how
   Gone off and left me lonely
   What am I supposed to do now

I meant to listen to you
   Hear the words you said
   Too busy forming counterarguments
   Here inside my head

I meant to pick up the phone
   Reach out and give you a call
   Got caught up in my life
   The hustle and bustle of it all

I meant to be a better person
   Think of others, not just myself
   Got caught up in the game of life
   Trying to be like everyone else

I meant to say a prayer
   Cast all my burdens at His feet
   Instead, I find myself depending on me
   No one to love, can't sleep, can't eat

I meant to take the time
    To remember why I mattered
    But here I stand in this moment
    Feeling completely and utterly shattered

I'm supposing it's too late for me
    To start now and finally do
    All those things I forgot at the time
    But I meant to

Joel 2:12-13; Matthew 11:28-30

My Faithful Best

No more of me to spread around
    Stretched thin, run into the ground

Rise to get the children up
    Warm the bottle, fill the cup

Make sure their bellies are all fed
    Get them to school, or daycare instead

Now my attention can turn to me
    For off to work I have to be

Hair, make-up, picture perfect
    Maybe not today, it ain't even worth it

From sunup to it's going down
    Everyone needs me to be around

Fixing problems, carrying burdens
    That are not mine, what if I'm hurting

Anxiety, confusion, depression, pain
    Constantly negative, no positive gain

Whether my sanity or another's pressed
    Living life in constant stress

They ask, "how are you" just to pull you in
    To tell you how awful their life has been

As the workday closes, I confess
    My life is good, cause theirs is a mess

Time to get the kids, work is done
    Nonstop chatter, new work just begun

Homework to do and mouths to feed
    Make time to play, insert time to read

Time for baths and planning for tomorrow
    No time for me, not one minute to borrow

Husband wants time at the days' ending
    No energy left, not even for pretending

Precious sleep and rest finally await
    But Lord, I forgot my time for you to make

Close my eyes, whisper a prayer
    Thank You for always being there

Weary is my mind, body, and soul
    You keep it all together, won't let me fold

You ease all the burdens cast on my shoulder
    In this quiet moment I lay them before you

You'll renew my strength as I enter into your rest
   I will wake up in the morning and do my faithful best. Selah

Hebrews 11:1

My Hope

Where does my Hope lie
   It's always rested with You
   I've leaned on You in dark times
   Every time You brought me through

As I climbed rough mountains
   Was baptized by fiery fountains
   You were with me in my spirit,
   Your voice, guiding me, I hear it

You are my forever hope

Through turmoil and loss
   You never left me alone
   When You made me a boss
   Through every triumph, every groan

When I wanted to give up the fight
   You were my guiding light
   I said I can't take anymore
   You led me through an open door

On the other side was peace
   Hope, love, joy and sweet release

Everything I need is always on the other side
To get there, I need You as my guide

I will always need my hope to get me through
My Hope will forever lie firmly in You
No other man or thing on Earth will do

You are my forever hope

Psalm 145:1-3

My Ministry

I accept my ministry to inspire, to teach
    To encourage curiosity in those I'm destined to reach
    Not a thirst for me perhaps; not even a hunger for college
    But create a desire to learn a deeper knowledge

Teach that what works for me may not work for you
    The understanding not in the how, but tied to the who
    Instructing that a life of contentment and abundance
    Can be realized amid all the chaos and the nonsense

It requires great attention and willingness to learn
    A heart that is open, a spirit willing to discern
    Each man or woman enrolling to complete the course
    Cannot come through coercion, no admission done by force

My class is open to all, and all are welcome to leave
    I greet you with love and my intent is not to deceive
    The content of the course sourced from only one reference
    It's stood throughout test of time, and it remains my preference

Men have tried to test it, debunk it, and deny it
    To all who are willing, I invite you to simply try it
    If it's not for you then I will say that I tried to plant the seeds
    Turn it over to the One who knows and understands your needs

1 Peter 4:10

My Son

I remember when we first met
　　Technically, you weren't here yet
　　But I felt something within me leap
　　When first I heard the sound, the beat

I'd heard the sound many times before
　　This time though, it touched my core
　　Never imagined my heart would quicken its pace
　　For someone nameless, without a face

But I knew you within that span of time
　　Bound together forever because you were mine
　　A mother I was destined to become
　　And you, my dear heart, would be my son

Soon we would meet face 2 face
　　Not in the most endearing or warmest place
　　Your cry was so soft, helpless, sweet
　　Black, curly hair perfect, you, unique

Only one you, chosen especially for me
　　For all of eternity my baby boy you'd be
　　How do I protect you from all yet to come
　　Keep dangers away, your protector, your mom

Dangers both seen and those I can't know
   How do I ensure safety wherever you go
   Now I realize the importance of understanding
   My role as a vessel to secure your safe landing

My part to teach you the things you must know
   To position as best as possible to help you grow
   For while we are bound to each other always
   You were never intended under my guidance to stay

You must one day return to the one who sent you here
   He will lead and direct you, and assuage all your fear
   I must allow Him to protect you under His shield
   As much as I want to direct you, I accept His will

I just had to write the words from a mother to her son
   When I met you I felt my life had just begun
   A brand-new start to get it right, My Sweet
   I love you always, My First Heartbeat

My Worth

Falling over myself to ensure a man knows my worth
    Need to start at the beginning, check myself first
    Do I know why I walk this bountiful earth
    All value wrapped up in him while all along I thirst

Sure, I love me some him, but to do so at my expense
    In what universe does that even begin to make any sense
    Saying I love you when I don't know how to love me
    If I could find my self-esteem, I'd reject your veiled misogyny

Raised to be downtrodden and broken
    Didn't get the memo, I'm too outspoken
    Devaluation of all that I know and am
    Dependent upon the value established by my man

Married now, what left to do but to take it
    Generational curse serious, but never too late to break it
    If he loves me, I'm supposedly under his protection
    If he is in order, I don't mind taken divine correction

All things are in order, then I'm falling in line
    Not contrary for liberation's sake, I can lead from behind (check my design)
    Only expecting what is due my rightful place on earth
    Not diminished to wifely duties, but the fullness of my worth

Proverbs 31:10-31

NO JUDGMENT

Am I responsible for me and you, too?
  Says who?

It's hard enough to get me right
  To deal with my plight

Why should I concern myself with your glory?
  I'm writing my own story

So, what, our stories intertwine?
  You get yours. I get mine.

I can't be concerned about what you do
  Though it may affect me too

I was born to live my life for me, not unselfishly
  What, you don't agree?

I don't want to watch you starve, die, or live in misery
  But is not that what it means to be free?

You should try harder, be better. You know, be like me.
  Self-made. All by myself, you see.

No time to rely on the fake goodwill of others. Oh no, not me!
   Don't need nobody.

Trusting people will cost you too much
   I ain't got time for such

My goal is not to hurt you, but I don't want to take a stand
   That's not in my plan

A world of hurt and pain comes from playing in that game
   I'm tapping out. No shame.

I'm trying to do what's best for me as a man
   Wouldn't expect you to understand
   Just doing the best that I can
   You are not a part of my plan

Philippians 2:3-8

No New Manual Needed

The next new book to fly off the shelf to help you to succeed
　　You'll be the first in line to buy it to get what you need

You're a hustler and you study life, the top one percent
　　What are they doing, what do they do to rise to their ascent

The playbook can't be that difficult, you too can follow all the rules
　　Just spell them out in a bestseller and you will work them like a mule

Manuals, step-by-step pamphlets might be good
　　But if the true answer is doing work, like any player should

Just like you, I am always open to a new lesson
　　But before you go too far, may I ask a simple question

Do we truly follow the instructions given by the authors
　　Or set aside the sage advice, because we're talkers, not true walkers

To hope for dreams unrealized and live life as a shot caller
　　One must put in work, face hardship, and know the hustle of a true baller

The conviction of your will to get after what is your heart's delight
　　Will take more than words on a page, from you it will take some fight

Not physical endangerment that causes one to harm or kill
But patience and endurance, strength of will, a true skill

The perfect instructions for success were given to us all so long ago
Guaranteed to ensure victory, the book from where all hopes flow

Repurposed and reimagined into books and all sorts of texts
People writing of their successes, us reading the secrets of their flex

I would challenge you to start with the original genuine manual
Some might give it the "OG" title, a nickname, a handle

It calls you to self-reflect, to love your fellow man
To honor what is good and true, it makes several demands

For all who hunger for the knowledge of how to be a boss
Who believe that they as soon as they achieve, here comes a loss

Those who feel disappointments and for knowledge they have a thirst
The first step in the original manual is simply, "Seek Ye First"
2 Timothy 2:15; Matthew 6:33

No Time to Be Quiet

The shy silent type, all my life polite
   Plenty I could've said, but my tongue I learned to bite.

Don't rumple any feathers or bother to rock the boat
   Voice another's opinion, then you become the scape goat

Don't start a disagreement; learn to go with the flow
   Everyone waiting for "yes", learning it's okay to say "no"

Don't start a conflict; Be seen as the angry other
   A label you won't shake, over your head it will forever hover

The practice of staying silent, never perfected by me truly
   Language is my lover, words - my constant companion, you see.

Foolish to think that somehow they would not fall from my lips in time
   Or randomly land on a blank page. My pen with ink still drips with rhyme

I've loved the flow of words since my youth and the power of their force
   The strength that they give to a young child who has not yet found their voice

The joy of learning to read fuels my success throughout this life of mine
   My plea to all mothers is gift your child with a love for reading, make the

time

I am finding that I am at my very best and can rest
    When I use the power of words to express
    The heavy burdens that exist deep in my chest

I want to keep them all to myself for who cares what I believe
    Remain a silent player in the game of life, but then they will not achieve

Something or someone is telling me to create within them a love affair
    Like I have with words. But can I take you there? Do I dare?

With words in my head, written on a page, or falling sweetly from my tongue
    Can we honor our elders and uplift our young

Who knows the answer? Nor you nor I, yet
    My soul implores me, this is no time to be quiet

Ecclesiastes 3:7

Not Forsaken

I have been young and now I am old
   I understand the prophecy which David foretold

No food on the table, no gas in the tank
   Yet never without, only God to thank

Miracles never ceasing to find me in times of need
   For those who are seeking, listen and take heed

Too youthful to know how to praise in my spirit
   Not listening to elders, no room in my heart to hear it

Knowing from when I was a little girl
   I wasn't as others who walk in this world

Protecting and guiding me through the ditches
   Helping me bat home runs at life's fast ball pitches

Clueless about the source of my victory
   Vain in believing it was me, but that's history

Not until I was living life in constant reaction
   Did I realize it was time to make a retraction

In the presence of my enemies, victory was won
Cup spilling over – what's going on?

I'm not doing any special living
But God has been blessing me, giving

All the earthquakes that should have had me shaken
Never once in my life was I left alone, forsaken

Foolish taking the accolades, believing the hype, and the praise
Dear God, it's all You, to the hills mine eyes I raise

Psalm 37:25-40

#3

Number 3
  Known to Buffalo, your city
  A stadium paralyzed, stood quietly

Number 3
  Reviving faith in humanity
  A nation collectively showing empathy

Number 3
  Prayers and thoughts this time sincerely
  Reached heaven, message received loudly

Number 3
  He said wherever 2 or 3
  Gather in His name he's in the midst with thee

Number 3
  Could it possibly be
  That in death you breathed life into many

Number 3
  We've never met, you and me
  But I thank God for your life, selfishly

Number 3
　Damar Hamlin, I humbly
　Thank you on behalf of all humanity

Matthew 18:20; John 11:40-44

Old School

An old school player
   For the new school slayer
   Sometimes aged things are fine

Do not need to be updated
   Reject being upgraded
   My quality is like that of red wine

Appreciate the new
   Like being among the few
   Understand the value I bring to the table

Do not want to be a sequel
   Know the merit of being unequaled
   Accept that not everyone is able

Old school is unique
   May leave some feeling weak
   Always willing to lead a master class

Love a young innovator
   Throwing shade on all the haters
   Who had the audacity to take them to task

Combining the old with the new
   A winning combination, true
   Though, it's hard to learn to give and take sometimes

Don't close your mind to what could be
   When you combine the power of you and me
   Given seasoned sparkle to contemporary shine

Passing Through

I've hidden my intentions
  Not out of spite or indecency
  Handling business as I should
  Keeping all eyes off of me

Navigating treacherous roads
  Climbing hills only meant for me
  Silent groans in my soul
  As I contemplate who I'm supposed to be

On a path leading to where
  Still remains a mystery of sorts
  Yet crystal clear in my mind
  My improbable mission, I can't abort

Troubles come and nights are long
  Want someone to help me bear the weight
  It gets so heavy, I stumble plenty
  The goal's insight, weariness abates

Do what I came to accomplish
  Before I can finish my course, my race
  Pass the knowledge to the next
  The others who wish to see His Face

Muddy waters getting clearer
   As I clear each checkpoint in sight
   Breathing easy, rest is near me
   Darkness giving way to light

A long journey's ending for this pilgrim
   Always knew this place not my home
   Peace abides and hope resides
   No need to mourn me when I'm gone

Soul's at rest, I'm at my best
   Finally made it to my Father's place
   He welcomed me home, never alone
   I've completed my necessary race

Matthew 11:28-30

Peace Be Still: The Storms of 2020

Father, help me this day. I pray.
　　I feel as though I'm losing my way.

All the lessons learned in my youth
　　Fading away, I need some proof.

I need to know that you're still here.
　　I can't deal with the hate and fear in my ear.

A killer among us, and we can't defeat it.
　　Sweeping all the Earth, history repeated.

A menace at home that continues to batter.
　　Shameful that we have to declare that our lives matter.

Witnessing murders daily in the news.
　　My children ask questions; I, too, am confused.

No one will listen, everyone too offended
　　Life, as we've known it completely, upended

So much confusion, so much fuss
　　The noise is so loud; it's drowning all of us

Even your children losing their way
  Dear God in Heaven, what should I pray?

The noise all around me, I'm starting to slide
  Never leave the house: gotta stay inside

All the noise and lies breaking my will.
  Nothing left to say, but *peace be still*

You spoke these words once in a storm; it obeyed
  Lord, we need you now; we are all dismayed

Repetitive whispers falling from my lips
  Peace be still, the enemy's grip begins to slip

I can feel anxiety and depression fading
  Mind clearing because on you I'm waiting

I lifted my eyes and my case I did make
  And you lifted us from this hypnotic state

Treasures on Earth destined to pass
  My hope in you will eternally last

When I needed the help of my Heavenly Father
  By the hands of my mind, He led me to the water

I found calm and peace, and His voice on the wind
  From out of my stupor, I did ascend

He reminded me that hate can't remedy hate
  Nor ignorance, ignorance, it will only war make

Our weapons of warfare all come from above
  The most powerful of these is merely to love

My peace now restored; marching orders received
  Ready to do battle because in Him I believe

Deuteronomy 20:4; Psalm 121; 2 Chronicles 7:14

P.O.W.E.R.

*P*rayer, the strength of my being
   It is my sight, when without seeing
   I find my way to my Father's place
   And He fills me with His love and grace

Open doors I could not budge on my own
   My Father opens all, never leaving His throne
   He opened my eyes so that I might see
   Everyone in this world need not be like me

Wisdom, I receive as each day passes
   Courage to discard my rose-colored glasses
   No longer must I weep with my face in my hands
   Crying about a world I wasn't meant to understand

Extraordinary in His gifts and His love for me
   Proof lies in the blood shed at Calvary
   Another like Him on earth, I shall not see
   Until the day when my savior comes for me

Riches and glory await me at home
   Where every day I will sit beneath His throne
   Right at His feet, my place is reserved
   To praise Him who loved me more than I deserved

Philippians 4:13

Piecing Me Together

We all have broken pieces
   Surely, that is by design
   Like a puzzle, overtime
   We find the pattern that binds

The piece that brings us joy
   That makes everything feel better
   For me, the sound of music
   Is what pieces me together

Another day don't delay
   Time to get up out of bed
   Water on my skin alive again
   Shake cobwebs out my head

Mary J, what did she say?
   As the mirror reflects my flaws
   Alicia Keys reminding me
   Even superwomen pause

Stop picking me apart

Make up done, I'm number one
   As Jennifer lets me know

I've got this and I can't miss
As I listen to Whitney blow

In my mind, I'm feeling fine
Lizzo telling me why
I'm special today in every way
I feel like I can fly

Piecing me together

More than words, that are heard
As my radio, blast a song
Lyrics say in every way
That I am fierce and I am strong

Joy or pain, sun or rain
It matters not, which comes my way
I will rejoice, I have no choice
Praise the Lord for my growth this day

Making me whole

Psalm 118:24

Poison: Release the Beast

Is resentment a beast to be unleashed?
  What is the danger of pent-up anger?
  Time wasted; bliss untasted
  Forfeited time; yours and mine
  Laughter muffled; feathers ruffled
  Hearts un-mended; souls untended
  Love buried deep; nights without sleep
  Pride unleashed, but so too, a beast
  Release the poison risen; learn to forgive them
  Proverbs 28:13; Colossians 3:13

Projection

Here come the projections
    From those who will undoubtedly bring the hate
    Sending all your failure and self-loathing,
    Like I don't already have enough on my plate
    Well, I do not wish to participate

"Who does she think she is"
    "She ain't no better than anybody else"
    The foolish nonsense you will spew
    Obviously in reference to yourself

"Anybody can write like that"
    "She probably stole it from another place"
    The things they say in threads on Twitter
    But rarely to the person's face

Like when Beyoncé song about a "Church Girl"
    Getting her groove on strong
    Good Christian folk lost their minds
    Condemning her to hell over a song

I could not help but wonder
    What was really going on?
    She is an entertainer spitting truth

Do we think the world can't see our wrongs

But when someone hits a nerve
   And calls us to the carpet
   We are wired to attack the person
   Instead of addressing the offensive topic
   Please, just stop it!

Galatians 5:25-26

Purpose Before Opinion (inspired by Jalen Hurts)

Waxes poetic, purpose before opinion
  Critics thought they'd figured you out
  But they don't have dominion

If only all knew the depth of which you speak
  Consider the human first wouldn't they?
  Their minds too weak

All born with a purpose no doubt
  Watching you work through your valleys
  Determined to figure it out

Mouths steady talking trying to speak into existence
  Foolishness and nonsense
  You'd already built up resistance

Opinions meaning nothing, fodder really
  Some hanging on to every word
  To most just sounding silly

J Hurts, still rolling with the tide
  A Sooner you'd become

For us, our joy, our pride

You knew you'd mount up with wings as an Eagle
    You knew your purpose
    In my humble opinion, regal

Proverbs 3:5-6; Psalm 32:8

Pushing Me

Pushing me to the edge
   Causing pains in my head
   Invisible punches that you throw
   Yet you act like you don't know

When I finally decide to leave
   Pretend that you're bereaved
   Like I'm the one who has deceived
   Despite all the crap I have received

Straining my senses
   I put up all my defenses
   Can't trust that you have my back
   Not with the way you act

When is enough, enough
   Haven't I proven that I'm tough
   Over the coals you continually rake
   I bend so much; you want me to break

But still, I stand here like stone
   Enduring this "love" until I'm gone
   Adoration is a bitch if this is it
   I feel the need to warn others quick

Steam dissipates as I settle down
    Face not so tense, absent the frown
    Rinse and repeat, we'll be here again
    Will I have the courage to put this to an END.

Red Flags

Silent sirens I cannot hear
   Just the lies whispered in my ear
   Flashing lights got me blinded
   Red flags in my head, constantly reminded

Think you got me on the ropes
   Trying to dash my little hopes
   Clutter in my head abounds
   Trying hard to pin me down

Red flags, trying to tell me something
   What I think I want, it ain't nothing
   If it's too easy leave it alone
   Disguised as fame, to pull me from the throne

If they want to take something that's mine
   I better check it, its value find
   If they want it, it's worth a lot
   Certain rights, that's all I've got

Red flags warn us if we adhere
   Don't ignore them, they'll disappear
   Only come again when I lose
   Cause I surrendered my right to choose

1 Corinthians 2:14

Run and Tell

Run and tell all my business
   It's my fault you even in this

Next time think I will keep my mouth closed
   Protect my thoughts that you can't wait to expose

You don't need any form of transportation
   To deliver negative conversation

I can't even complete the full sentence
   Your fingers itching to push "send it"

Lost my job, arguing with my man
   Didn't make the line, your mouth you ran

Kid off to prison, I can't read, can't cook
   All of my business headlined on Facebook

Deepest secrets with you I entrust
   But I'm juicy gossip to fill your lust

I can save my postage fees spent on the mail
   I got a few things you can run and tell

God is blessing me in so many ways, I lost count
  Searching social media, nobody pushed that out

Promotion at the job, increase in money to bat
  There's some gossip. Go, chat that

My man's all over me, children successful
  Go tell that. Ain't that a mouthful?

Tell my age and how it glows on this beautiful brown
  Tell how I take a punch and bounce back from the ground

While you are at it, surely there is something He's done for you
  If I were you, I'd run and tell that, too.

Psalm 71:17

Said the Queen

Said the beautiful Queen to her handsome King
    Let's build this kingdom together
    I will reign by your side, my love
    Not as your servant, but your helper

For this is how it was intended to be
    Since our time began
    But many have listened, unwisely
    To the proclamations of man

If we lean on each other
    When we are weak to gain the other's strength
    We will find that the bond between us will grow
    For this is how it was meant

To be my husband, my lover, and my friend
    To see what others will never see
    To be your wife, your confidante, and your muse
    To bare your children willingly

To learn and know the secrets
    That will cement our lives together
    To build health and wealth and memories
    That will last throughout our forever

No man, no woman, no outside words
    Should determine our fate, just us
    We will focus on one another
    This is how we will build our trust

Said the queen to the king
    If true love is what we seek
    No other's opinions matter
    Loyalty to one another we must keep

We will leave the world on the outside
    This is our home that we build
    When problems come to our door
    We will not give them audience – they must yield

We will seek advice from the great advisor
    Who knows all and who sees
    This is how we will build our kingdom
    My King, hear me, please

We will maintain the order
    That is impossible for some
    Here in our kingdom, my King
    The Lord's will must be done

1 Corinthians 14:40

Scenery

His favorite scenery, no surprise
    Gazing lovingly at me, as I rise
    Looking in my soft brown eyes
    As if he sees his soul in mine, mesmerized

When he looks at me I know
    I am the only lady in his show
    Where I walk his eyes will go
    So, I sway my hips, real, real, slow

He smiles at me as he looks
    He reads me like his favorite book
    Cast his rod, Lord knows, I'm hooked
    Steaming gaze – got me shook

Now sitting still, I strike a pose
    His soft, lovely, delicate rose
    Here beside him, the one he knows
    Perhaps the scenery should lose the clothes

Song of Solomon 4:7

Seeds of Doubt

Dropping around me everywhere
  Seeds of hopelessness and despair
  Seems like time's running out
  Surrounded by seeds of endless doubt

Chasing after something distant, aloof
  I know it's there, but have no proof
  Running, but my feet not moving
  Tired of feeling like I am always losing

Got to free myself from this ghost town
  Legs caught up in the sand, I'm sinking down
  Pretend they don't hear me, ignore my cry
  Friends, family, acquaintances, all walking by

Slipping away, seeds of doubt taking root
  Come on, be strong, don't eat from its fruit
  Almost there, I feel it. I know it.
  Bones growing weary. Limp body doesn't show it.

But I see the light shining in the distance
  Making me stand tall, I will not be resistant
  I accept the light and all its assurance
  Shaking off seeds of doubt, replace with endurance

Hope in the wind, mercy in the rain
   Storms blessing my soul, healing all pain
   I hear a knock. The door I gladly open
   I search no more, it's the ONE for whom I was hoping.

Hebrews 11:6; Revelation 3:20-21

Selfie

What is this fascination I have with me
    Chasing self-perfection continually

The pressure of it all too much really
    The only way I know to live - behind my Selfie

They know I'm using filters shamelessly
    To create the image, I want all to see

Right pose, right smile, right tilt, it's got to be
    Before I can post this flawless selfie

If I undress for all to see
    For the sake of argument, if I lived unselfishly

What would life look like, what would it be
    If you knew my weakness, my vulnerability

Would you reach out a hand to help lift me
    Or would you exploit what I already deem to be ugly

My scars, my wounds, that part of me too friendly
    Would you rip me to shreds and try to end me

Suppose I will never know, it's much too scary
So, I will hide beneath the filter, the Selfie —- all you need to see

Simply Complicated

What makes something simple
   The ability to understand it
   The ability to deconstruct it
   Or the ability to command it

Life, so complicated
   By all these contradictory rules
   Seemed intentionally designed
   To make us all look like fools

At first couldn't decipher
   Couldn't detect any meaning
   Whether studying quietly at home
   Or while the choir is divinely singing

Living abundantly and rich
   To give everything away
   Accepting me as I am
   But judging every word I say

Coming as I am
   Into my Father's house
   Eyes undressing me at the door
   Leave me feeling like a louse

Why should the simple be complicated
   By the men who are so smart
   Instead of searching with the spirit
   Intent on using head and heart

Complicating matters written
   Plain as day before our eyes
   So simple are the rules for us
   We feel compelled to compromise

Such tragedy in our stories
   And while you may debate it
   Too often we take that which is simple
   And twist it until it is simply complicated

1 Timothy 2:3-4; James 1:5

Sit in Silence

Don't say anything
  Just sit and wring your hands
  Turn and look away
  Never learn to take a stand

Pray the problems away
  Pretend they will never become yours
  Assume they'll always find their way
  And land at someone else's doors

Sit in silence and hope
  That the world all around you
  Will hold itself at bay as you ignore it
  As if not incumbent upon what you do

Protect only your beloved
  As if we are not all connected
  Turn your back, close your eyes
  One day, you, too will be affected

But for now, enjoy tainted peace
  Happiness and abundance laced in violence
  Experienced at the expense of another's suffering
  While you continue to sit in silence

Job 15:31

Solo Artist

How do "we" start this
 I'm a blessed solo artist

Get there quicker on my own
 No time to spare, work better alone

Better when I am free to breathe
 Not wearing your feelings on my sleeve

It doesn't bother me if you want to leave
 Fine with me. Do it. Please.

When I go solo no one sees
 Days of distress, nights on my knees

When I work solo no one hears my pleas
 Asking God's mercy for the least of these

When I walk solo, I don't have to explain
 What many may view as a life lived in vain

When I keep it solo there are no egos to deny
 For I have a TRIO on which I rely

My solo act may look selfish to you
   I invite you to look from a different view

I've never been solo doing anything of worth
   So grateful my TRIO has known me since birth

It may seem a fallacy or contradiction
   For you to understand this world I live in

But don't judge my solo act when I rise or fall
   My TRIO has my back, sees me through it all

I embrace the act of walking in my truth, on my own
   For though a solo artist, I never walk alone

John 1:1-14; John 14:26

Someone's Waiting for You

No time to relax
  Too much to do
  You've contemplated enough
  Someone's waiting for you

Holding up life
  Holding up works
  Pausing progression
  Hoping for perks

Don't worry about rewards
  Don't be concerned about pitfalls
  Your path is such as it is
  He has an answer for it all

There will be winding roads
  Some will be slippery when wet
  Yield and stop signs
  Will await you, don't fret

None of that matters
  Proceed to the route
  Your precious cargo awaits
  Time to go in pursuit

Someone's waiting for you
   And what only you can give
   They're dying for your arrival
   So, you can show them how to live

1 Peter 5:1-5

Stand and Deliver

You want me to stand and deliver
    Bring the masses to their feet
    Turn stone into silver
    Take your mess, make it sweet

Be the doormat on which others trod
    Take one or all for the team
    Be oblivious to the wink and nod
    Keep chasing the not-made-for-me dream

Become the go-to guru
    The one who knows it all
    Work my mystical, made-up voodoo
    The wisest person on the hall

If I don't stand and deliver
    Then what, pray tell will come of us
    Am I supposed to start to quiver?
    Think that we all will turn to dust?

My replacement waits in the wings
    To fill my seat before its cold
    Cause I, like all things,
    Will slow with time, as I grow old

Or do I dare put my value to test
   Do I show that I have opinions too
   Introduce that I am not voiceless
   Will you still be the true blue?

You want me to stand and deliver
   Until I have something to say
   Then your anger makes you shiver
   And you want me to go away

With a voice, I'm not useful to the team
   I'm a liability, fade into the background
   Found someone quiet to deliver the dream
   My role now, to sit and not make a sound

Matthew 5:14-16

Stay In Your Lane

Not fun anymore?
  What exactly were you looking for?

Living a dream not yours
  Suddenly feels like doing chores

Never your fame
  You thought it a game
  Hopping in someone else's lane
  Need someone to blame for your shame

Failure all around town
  Still lost, never found

Always wanting to taste
  Hell-bent on trying to replace

A dream not made for you
  It ain't coming true

All the jealousy
  Aimed directly at me
  Pure insanity

For something never meant to be

Self-inflicted pain
    There'll never be any gain
    Try staying in your lane

Triumph there you will find
    In due time

Trying to bump me off the road
    While lugging your heavy load

Stressing to live life on top
    By crowding my lane, has to stop
    I've put up roadblocks

Do not enter my lane.
    This is insane.

Ecclesiastes 4:4

Sustah to Sister

If you're my sister then can't we disagree
   Is it a must that I see the world the way that you see
   Isn't it enough that you are forever a part of me
   Bound by this selfless love through all eternity

Part of an upbringing and tight knit family
   Yet somehow jaded by greed, ruined by jealousy
   All I ever wanted, you are the epitome
   Pride blocks the zenith of our preordained destiny

Sustah 2 Sister, no one understands you, but me
   Stare at my reflection, wonder if I'll ever be
   The fullness and richness, all the possibility
   Made of our Creator, fearfully, wonderfully

Sustah 2 Sister will you ever love me genuinely
   Wanting to embrace one another, surveying each other cautiously
   Daring to learn to trust my image staring back at me
   For you were my Sister then and my Sustah you shall forever be
   2 Corinthians 13:5, 8-9; Romans 12:2-5

Temper Me

Temper me Father, today, I pray
  To love your children, not as I want, but as You say

They try my spirit and my weary mind
  Stretch to the limit, all in me that is decent and kind

I know I am imperfect with faults of my own
  But, hateful, mean-spirited? Nah, I leave that alone

Disrespectful of elders, disregarding of self
  Why should I think for a minute, they care for someone else?

Wanting to help them, meet them where they are
  But they push the limits of decency, sometimes going too far

Forgive me Father my weakness and please hear my complaint
  May Your will be done through me; let me mount up and not faint

Isaiah 40:31

Thank You

Peace, solace, and gratitude
  Today, no misplaced attitude

Just thankful for the gift
  Tonight, it came to me, swift

Stumbling, falling, tripping everyday
  Carrying, lifting, holding me all the way

Crying, scratching, fighting through it all
  Laughing, gripping, clinging to the wall

Like the bug on my windshield, splattered
  Million pieces everywhere, feeling so battered
  But still I mattered.

Somehow I still dare to be bold
  Because I know You will make me whole

Basking in the fullness of Your love
  I feel it from above

Tonight, Your perfect peace
  Grants me sweet release

Thank You for my gift
   I promise as I climb, I will lift

Romans 8:31

The Beauty of Legacy

Alabama the beautiful
  She has been dutiful
  The world ready and willing to receive
  The works her best would achieve

From out of the sticks and dirt
  Came extraordinary work
  While all minds and thoughts affixed to slavery and cotton
  The wonders she sent forth, almost forgotten

Prayer and love seeds planted
  Almost taken completely for granted
  The world's picture of us, slanted

Ignorance, illiteracy, backwoods
  Terms we understood, not meant for good
  Elevated, placed in the spotlight
  To obscure our wisdom and our might

For some treasures must be hidden
  In plain view, to avoid derision
  Until such a day is come
  When the will of the Almighty must be done

From Jesse Owen's track and field run
   Running for gold, lifting daughters and sons
   Had no idea what he'd just begun

To Bo Jackson and the fields that he plowed
   Feet running fast, bat cracking loud
   Football, baseball – hear those cheering crowds
   At one point, not allowed

Octavia Spencer acting as the "Help"
   "Hidden Figures", a secret from us kept
   When I learned they existed, I wept

Coretta Scott would marry a King
   You know the one, he had that dream
   But in the background, she was maintaining everything

Hank Aaron, Joe Louis, Condoleezza Rice
   Zora Neale Hurston, Claudette Colvin, all paying the price
   Satchel Paige, Willie Mays all breaking the myth
   Making good trouble like Congressman John Lewis

Percy Lavon Julian, Joseph Lowery, Rosa Parks, so many more
   Terri Sewell, Autherine Lucy, all waiting for you to explore
   The legacy of Alabama and all that they lived and live for
   So, you can rise up and walk through it, that wide open door

Too many names to list on this page
   None disrespected, but homage to all paid
   We must honor their legacy, the building blocks that they laid

Your thoughts and your actions are part of the reason
    You hold yourself back and you live in your dead season
    Your roots run deep if you only believe them
    Know your past, see your dreams, now get up and achieve them

Romans 15:4-7

The Body Politic

My body – a political object
  To be defined by who?
  My choice – not mine at all
  If left up to you.

An organized body
  To determine how my person should function
  And now ignore me, too?
  The gumption.

Who should get to decide
  How I choose to live my life?
  If I don't trample on your rights
  Should not my choice suffice?

We talk of Liberty
  Freedom of will for every man.
  But always with exceptions
  Man, can't we grandstand?

Of course, you presume
  To know what is best for all
  Tell me how to live, to die
  The unmitigated gall

I can birth and raise children
    Pay taxes and work the hold daylong
    But make a choice for which you disagree
    Automatically I must be wrong

Living by your logic
    I would swear that I am insane.
    How do I manage to walk around
    With this feeble woman's brain?

Romans 13:1-8

The Color of Being Human

If I choose my color appropriately
  Will it make you approve of me
  What if this choice is not mine at all
  But a circumstance by which I stand or fall

If I choose a color of the rainbow
  Will it make you stand with me, or your frustrations grow
  If I choose red, or yellow, or blue
  What would these colors mean to you

If the red of rage is the color I wear
  Does that turn you on and make you more aware
  Or is the yellow of cowardice more appeasing to you
  Giving you control over all that I say and do

If I choose the blue of an officer or of a nurse
  Would you bless my existence, or my life would you curse
  If I wore the green of my envy upon my sleeve
  Would you stay to befriend me, or would you hasten to leave

Or is it the green of paper and silver of coins
  That truly ignites the fire burning in your loins
  Consuming the spirit from taking perfect effect
  Gold overwhelming your senses, commanding all your respect

Maybe it isn't color that causes judgments to be made
  More precisely we should consider not color, but shade
  If I should choose black or it's opposite, white
  Which one would be to your delight

The pigment that shadows and colors my skin
  More influential than the light or darkness that flows from within
  More powerful than the crimson blood we share
  These artificial tones that cause such despair

The strength of my conviction not alive in my integument
  Yet scripted to reveal the heights of my relevance
  Concocted delusions that paint an unflattering picture
  Eyes only seeing the mind's distorted villainous caricature

I'm rewriting this narrative for those who will accept
  While I love my shade, it's my inner man that is adept
  I work from within, but you see from without
  I exist in the fullness of me, and I wish to leave no doubt

1 Samuel 16:7; Proverbs 23:7; 2 Corinthians 4:16

The Comforter

Oh brother, David
   Kindred spirit of mine
   I understand why you wrote the Psalms
   Praising the Divine
   Impossible to stop
   Telling of the Joy and peace of mind
   When words to explain Him
   Have not yet been defined

He sent to me the Comforter
   To get me through impossible times
   Were it not for His grace and love
   I know I'd lose my mind
   I have to tell the world
   Repeat it a million times
   In the only way I know how
   Threw my pen, by these rhymes

The Comforter, He knows me
   When words I cannot find
   To describe the sorrow and the madness
   He brings His peace on time

Others stumbling all around me

Hustling through the grind
Consumed with fear and anxiety
Animosity and hate, their days defined

Not that I don't feel these things
Sometimes all combined
But the Comforter arrests them all
And allows me peace to find

Always gonna write of His greatness
Sing of how He tames my wandering mind
Keep your worldly comforts and pleasures
I'll take the Comforter's peace every time

John 14:16-18

The Courage to Feel

How does one examine the ability to feel?
  Is it prerequisite for those serving to heal?

When the physical is cared for and we've no more control
  Life hangs in the balance and hands we gently hold, trying to console

Silent prayers we say — sometimes aloud
  Never wanting to offend; playing to the crowd

Is it not the compassion that lies within us all
  That allows us to answer whatever the call

To listen intently or just be aware
  That at any given moment, we are called on to care

Not physical, sociocultural, or even mental lessons learned
  In books and classes from the degrees we've all had to earn

Some certainly argue compassion cannot be taught
  I will counter it's too valuable to be forsaken or bought

No price tags on lives worth the entire world's treasure
  Right decisions, wrong reasons, how do we truly measure

Only those who wear the titles and do the work of a healer
  Will ever know the genuineness of the heart, in some moments, no concealer

For all who are blessed with the power to heal
  It is my prayer you never take for granted the courage to feel

As difficult a task this, at times, may be to see through
  We are truly appreciative and thank you for the caring each of you do

2 Corinthians 1:3-4

In dedication to all nurses everywhere, that ever was and will be. But especially to those graduates of the Ira D. Pruitt Division of Nursing at The University of West Alabama and the Capstone College of Nursing at The University of Alabama.

The Intangible You

Who are you, really?
　Who are you meant to be?
　Questions we sometimes ask ourselves
　But do we contemplate them in sincerity

Are you afraid of the answer
　Does it cause uneasiness, concern
　Examining the intangibles that make you, you
　Aren't you curious to learn?

Are you an inquisitive being
　Observant of all that is around
　Or are you oblivious to everything
　Not impressed by sight, touch, nor sound

Are you brutally honest by nature
　Is integrity an integral part of you
　Or does truthfulness pale in comparison
　To the many favors that others can do

Does compassion drive your days?
　Are you even aware of flaws within yourself
　Or do you prefer the juiciest gossip
　Being disseminated about everyone else

Who exactly are you
   Isn't it time that you begin to find out
   In case you don't know where to start
   Perhaps you begin by asking about

How do others describe you
   Not the things they can see and can touch
   But those things that take no shape or form
   Things that "impress" them so much

While maybe unpleasant at first
   It may prove an informative exercise
   Leaving you some food for thought
   But hopefully, leaving you pleasantly surprised

Do they see you as you see yourself
   The answer, some may fear it
   Take it all with a grain of salt
   For you should be your most honest critic

The invisible parts of you
   Known as "soft skills" in the world I entertain
   Hard for some to understand their relevance
   But may open a door or a career maintain

Never too late to take inventory
   Collect the data points and review
   All the traits, both good and not
   That manifest in the Intangible You

Proverbs 10:9

The Messenger

Chosen to bring you a message
  By way of my words and my voice
  Receive it or not, not up to me
  That is totally your choice

My role clearly defined
  To simply deliver words to you
  My job to give you the knowledge
  It's up to you to follow through

Stop blaming my God
  For the destruction man caused
  Don't understand what I'm saying
  Think about it for a moment. Pause.

Desiring God to do miracles for you
  Want Him to grant us grace
  Pick up the Book and do your part
  Bow your head and seek His face

Hard to trust in that you cannot see
  Barely like what's in front of your face
  Study to show yourself approved
  The only way you can keep pace

I know what it is to be lonely
    To have nights where I've forsaken sleep
    Imploring God for answers
    Wondering if His promises He'd keep

Many years He's walked with me
    Many ups and downs along my road
    But every time I thought I could do no more
    He always lightened my load

Many years it took me to gain
    A firm and faithful understanding
    This life of mine, I think I'm in control
    But it's all in God's time and planning

No need to be envious of others' talents
    In another's gifts I can rejoice
    Blessed with talents and gifts of my own
    Not of my choosing – not my choice

Probably got you shaking heads now
    Twisting lips and turning up noses
    I'm battle-tested and dressed in armor
    Prepared to receive thorns instead of roses

My gift perfectly designed
    For the role I would play one day
    To be a messenger for the King
    And place His love on full display

Proverbs 13:17

The Road There

Stuck in my head those things my parents said
    And not that they weren't true, especially from their point of view
    But when is it time to examine to possibly reimagine
    A history of loathe and despise through compassion's eyes
    Bitter pill to begin to swallow but living in bitterness leaves us hollow
    Gotta find a better way to mend fences, if the plan is redemption
    All of us are suffering from past sins, all those fears and pains we hold within
    Refuse to see others through love's lens, the only power that will begin the cleanse
    Perhaps we prefer this life we live, easier when nothing's expected, nothing to give
    Who wants to work for peace's sake when each other's will we break
    Who has time to find forgiveness when I wake so I can live this
    Only when man opens his mind will he eventually find
    What has been there the entire time, love's light trying to shine
    The road there has a predictable map, on which has been laid many a trap
    Not willing to read it or learn, but with this ridiculous hate and fear, we burn

Luke 14:21-23

The True Enemy

Is the true enemy, not the one I see?
　　Could my true enemy really be me?

Been relying on these eyes of mine to identify
　　What only my spiritual prowess will allow me to spy

What if these spirits and principalities
　　Lying beneath skin and nationalities

The point I'm trying to make to the mob
　　Let's not give outside factors credit for an inside job
　　Fixated on the skin of our sisters and brothers
　　Bound and determined to label them 'other'
　　If they're 'no good', then call them no good
　　Whether living in the White House, the suburbs, or the hood

Let's not hate and loathe foes in our mind
　　While the spirit implores us to seek out villains of a different kind
　　Lord God in Heaven, please help us discern and decline
　　This madness we've allowed mankind to define
　　The destruction of other humans under the guise of the divine
　　This spiritual wickedness in high places, a drug that we savor as a fine wine
　　An inheritance of brutality and corruption, we can cease at any time

Black on black we dare not bring to light those crimes
 A traitor to the race if you speak the truth, just toe the line
 White people using black people as targets, making headlines
 We must speak against all manner of evil, the only way to climb

Father, turn us from this world's distractions like Saul make us blind
 Until we see and hear You only, and our foolish ways we leave behind
 The world is so disconnected, but I'm clinging to the True Vine.

John 15:1-17

Time to Grow Up

She's really gone
  She's not coming back
  She no longer can cover-up
  Blemishes in areas where you lack

It's time to grow up
  Past time, long overdue
  When answers are needed now
  They're gonna come looking for you

So, what if you slip up
  Don't think you won't make mistakes
  That means you're still learning
  But you have everything it'll take

Handpicked for this occasion
  You were chosen for a reason
  Stop limiting your potential
  The harvest is ripe, this is your season

She told you who you were
  Instilled in you to whom you belong
  "Okay, Mama, I miss you so
  Now it's my time to show you weren't wrong"

Time to Take Time

If we can't get time back
  Then why do we yield it so fast
  Shouldn't we be more thoughtful
  With something so precious that doesn't last

Shouldn't we use time more wisely
  To ponder the consequences of our choices
  To not nonchalantly respond to matters
  By way of manipulative voices

Wouldn't you value a day you had not seen
  If you knew you'd never see it again
  Yet every day we blow away life
  And precious moments like time will never end

Couldn't time be used to consider our history
  To create present peace and harmony
  Or am I a fool to believe it true
  That we waste time and life needlessly

Without the benefit of our toys and gadgets
  Would we have more time to ponder and think
  Could we hold uncomfortable, honest conversations
  That wouldn't have to happen in a blink

Would we understand that some things take time
    They take patience to ensure their done right
    Not everything has a set timetable
    Not everything must end in a fight

The world - always in a hurry
    Exactly where are we trying to go
    Still, we haven't got there running fast
    Surely, we can stop, at least move slow

If we take time to take time back
    To enjoy things as we did once before
    Could we find time to love one another
    Or do those times exist no more

Proverbs 21:5; Romans 13:11

To The Make-Believe Sisters

To the make-believe sisters, you know who you are
   Pretend you're on my side, set this make-believe bar
   Gotta rock the right clothes, drive the right car
   Such tired, shallow "standards", only get you so far

If I don't wear a certain color, ready to go to work
   Underhanded "compliments", I see your crooked smirk
   How much time does it take, perfecting your inner jerk
   Fronting like you chilling, I see you lurk

Waiting to see me fall down so you can discover "what"
   Do I bruise when I'm hurt, do I bleed when I'm cut
   For all of your jokes want me to be the butt
   But every time I'm winning you keep your mouth shut

Thank you for being true to us showing your true side
   Reminding me why I refuse to let the "little things" slide
   Behind your "charity" to others you always want to hide
   Couldn't be a make-believe sister even if I tried

1 Corinthians 4:7; Isaiah 3:16-17

The Gift

I am the gift
　　That keeps on giving
　　Finding joy and peace
　　In daily living

What incredible thing
　　Will I do today?
　　Will it be what I write
　　What I build, what I say?

Not to focus on my prowess
　　But free us both from the stress
　　Of competing with another goddess
　　Of whom I truly think no less

Why try to compete
　　With someone who is not me
　　Such a vain and ridiculous
　　Place for us to be

Live in your brilliance
　　And I will live in mine
　　Compete with yourself
　　No time to waste standing in line

James 1:17

Thought and Prayers

Thoughts and prayers
  So many sheets and layers

What's in your thoughts?
  The guns that were bought?
  The massacre, the onslaught?

Maybe the victims' faces
  All the unsafe places
  The once ago sacred gathering spaces

Synagogues, schools, churches
  Stores visited to make a simple purchase

Clubs, casinos, and bars
  All now places for domestic wars.

Didn't mention the hospital rooms
  All in our thoughts, all doomed

What's in your prayers?
  The hope that nobody cares.
  Owning a gun may create scares?

Pain, sadness, numbness
   Is there any courage among us?

Too much to pray for some action
   No? Not any? Not even a fraction?

We pray for souls lost
   But we shrug at the cost

Pray for hearts left to mourn
   Pray for those yet to be born
   Pray for peace, get your scorn
   No solutions. Divided. Torn.

Thoughts and prayers – seem disgraceful
   A phrase with no meaning – how hateful

Adding to the suffering and the pain
   Have we no honor, no shame

To offer a thought and a prayer
   But do nothing, show you don't care

As faith without works is dead
   So are the empty words you just said

Words without action
   A useless distraction

So sad, so true
   Pray no one has to offer you
   Empty thoughts and insincere prayers for a love you once knew.

Matthew 6:5; Luke 18:10-14

Too Late

I hope I'm not too late
   While I was taking my sweet time
   Trying to get myself together
   Figuring out a life, not completely mine

I pray I'm not too late
   That I didn't wait too long
   Didn't realize that in your weakness
   You were waiting for me to be strong

I must not be too late
   For how could I forgive myself
   Wasting precious moments
   Should've been caring for someone else

It is not too late
   For these words to find your heart
   To renew within your spirit
   The kindling of a brand-new start

I feel it is not too late
   For you to realize that a new day
   Is just beyond the horizon
   Don't listen to the negative words they say

He is never too late
   He has always been on time
   And He has lit a fire in me
   To share Him with you through the gift of rhyme

Proverbs 16:9; 2 Peter 3:8-9

Too Much

Too much procrastination
   Too much information

Too much screen time
   Too much invading my mind

Too much money to spend
   Too much with which to contend

Too much gluttonous food to eat
   Too much commotion interrupting my sleep

Too much fine jewelry to wear
   Too much clothing, we don't care

Too much unnecessary stuff
   Too much, but never enough

Blessed or cursed with all I desired
   Because now that I have it, much is required

Conditioned to collect all I can get
   When it makes me less humane, is it too much, yet

TOO MUCH

Luke 12:47-48

Turbulence

Turbulence not on a plane. But in my brain.
　　Shaking me to my soul, starting to feel cold

Thoughts are indecisive
　　Those surrounding me divisive

What I thought to be is no more
　　Instinct to keep them out, slam every door

Needing silence to negotiate the violence
　　Need peace of mind. There is none to find.
　　Not here.

Release from this turbulence.
　　Creating this massive disturbance.

Volcano ready to erupt
　　Like an earthquake, but abrupt

Quiet. Still. Rest. Calm.
　　Breathe. Release. Feel the balm.
　　No fear.

Eyes closed. Mind open to consider

Release the thoughts infiltrating. Bitter.

Tears streaming like lava, let them fall
Say good-bye to the sadness of it all.

Body shaking from the quake inside
Let go of animosity and foolish pride
Setting up residence, ready to abide
Listen, you're near.

Your race is not over, you're not finished
Need time to reflect. Room to replenish.

Arise. Embrace. Find favor in this place.
Mind, body, spirit need a rejuvenating space.
To release the turbulence.

Psalm 46:1

Unapologetic

At the end of each day as we settle down
  And we look back at how we faced it
  Are there moments that we inevitably replay
  Then pause and wish we could erase it

Saying things and doing things
  Designed to initiate pain or harm
  Not meant to elevate or move forward
  Or bring positivity to anyone

Bumping into others on the street
  Passing them in the hall, throwing 'bows
  Not moving over, or opening your mouth
  Because it hurts to simply say, "hello"

Wanting things from others
  They would never get from you
  Showing up late to obligations
  Sometime with extras in your crew

Unapologetic about anything
  Because you are merely doing you
  And boldly living your best life
  As you were 'purposed' to do

Just a word of caution as you live
    And navigate your days
    Unfazed by others in your path
    Unconcerned about the effects of your ways

Someone is watching and taking note
    As you glide through life apathetic
    Not too late to renegotiate
    Is it wise to always be unapologetic

James 5:16

Walking in Her Glow

Five long years have passed
   Still learning to live without your laugh
   I am trying to get past
   Most days I wear the mask
   But I wish that you were here

For you never got to see
   The fullness of your legacy
   What would in time come to be
   My plans for you and me
   But fate made it perfectly clear

I had to learn to carry on
   Though everything felt so wrong
   My biggest fan long gone
   Your voice alive inside a phone
   The memory of our bond cannot be broken

The sacred love of a mother and child
   All the hurt, you made seem mild
   Reminding me that my life's worthwhile
   Replacing my tears with your loving smile
   In your presence words didn't need to be spoken

This tribute bares no regret
   For I do not wish to fret
   About the mother that I get
   To remember and to set
   Within the indelible portrait of adoration in my spirit

I was blessed beyond the earth
   Since the day of my birth
   You taught, your Penny, all my worth
   To believe that I deserved to be first
   Thank you for making me be still and know and hear it.

I do not want these words to end
   It feels like departing from you again
   And though my heart is on the mend
   Tears still come, sorrow still descends
   I know that you needed your rest

I simply want the world to know
   What it looks like to walk in a mother's glow
   To love your children and allow them to grow
   Because your playbook's rules I did follow
   Mama, I miss you so. I'm still walking, though.
   I'm doing my best
   I love you Mary Catherine.

Ephesians 6:1-2

We the People

We the people, an ideal, a hope
   Seem so simple, but heavy in scope
   If I question the sincerity, you call me a "dope"
   Let me explain for those who'll label me "woke"

We the people, a foundation
   We the people, a new nation
   We the people, needs explanation
   Not all the people part of the congregation

We the people, some not included
   We the people, the American dream eluded
   We the people, feels diluted
   Most of the people left out, excluded

We the people, don't dare defend it
   We the people, yes, since amended
   We the people, some still offended
   The American family mixed, blended

We the people seeking a perfect union?
   We the people, then what are we doing?
   We the people, establish Justice?
   We the people, for who among us?

We the people, ensure domestic peace?
    We the people, but not to those who are least?
    We the people, providing defense?
    To the enslaved, sounds like nonsense.

We the people, promote the general welfare?
    We the people, but that requires you to care.
    We the people, secure the BLESSING of liberty?
    Yet we the people wouldn't set men free.

We the people, powerful words for
    We the people to learn to adore.
    We the people - slave, women, and poor
    Not the people for many years more.

We the people, fought numerous fights
    To claim our inalienable rights.
    We the people, still questioning my worth
    To be a full citizen in the place of my birth.

We the people brought against our will
    But for we the people, the battle has been uphill
    We the people want to be perfectly clear
    We are the people, and we belong here.

Trying to exist without having to explain
    That l was not the people in that sweet refrain.
    Still the thought brings unwanted pain
    And we have to debate this? No, not again.

1 Timothy 2:1-2; Galatians 4; Exodus 14:14

What Are You Waiting For

Maybe tomorrow will be better
    You will be ready by then
    Today is not a good day anyway
    It is not your time to begin

Everyone else is so much better
    Their road much easier than yours
    Let them build a way first, do the work
    Do not bore yourself with such chores

You can watch all the moves they make
    And fake it, until you decide to show
    You can't be expected to do as others do
    They understand your pace is slow

You don't have much to offer right now
    You would just be in their way
    Summer is coming soon
    While they work, they won't mind if you play

They know how you love to travel
    To dance by the beat of the ocean
    Go and secretly dine with good friends
    No need to cause a commotion

No one will know you are not here
    You cannot contribute much
    You'll be back just in time
    To help put on the finishing touch

You'll take your seat at the table
    When all of the work is complete
    Pretend that your hand was all up in it
    Such a marvelous feat

No need for life to pass everyone by
    Hard work can be such a bore
    You know there's more fun in living life
    You don't know what we're waiting for

James 2:24-26

What I Allow

No need to complain or fuss or whine about my circumstance
  Considering I do little to intervene whenever I'm given a chance

No violence or nasty words or bad wishes must I bestow
  Upon those who want to take me down to my lowest low

I can keep my head in the game and their foolishness disavow
  For I have learned they can make me do no more than that which I allow

How many times I've said, "they made me want to act a fool"
  They don't have that kind of power, unless I give them rule

The power of self-control and self-determination
  Eliminates much harmful stress and needless situations

What I allow and who I allow to control my thoughts and actions
  Will determine the road I travel if it has destruction and distractions

Take control of your life and never let another decide your fate
  Don't let time expire, do it before it's too late

Proverbs 25:28

Who's Left to Love Me

If I should let you go
   Allow you to be free
   Whatever shall I do
   Who's left to love me

You were the only one
   Who understood my ways
   Didn't try to change me
   On my especially bad days

Always knew I'd come around
   Saw the hidden part of me
   That part that no one knows
   Simply 'cause they chose not to see

You told me I could soar
   Move mountains stubbornly standing still
   I had no strength to move them
   But they crumbled inexplicably at your will

Dark, scary winding roads
   That I know lay menacingly ahead
   I can't walk them alone
   The mere thought feels me with dread

Too much left for us to do
    I don't want you to go
    Too much left to tell you
    The secrets I want only you to know

If you leave me now
    What would you have me do
    I suppose you loved me well enough
    I should let you go and love you, too

Lamentations 3:32, Revelation 21:4

Why

So many ask this question about so many things
  If birds can fly, why can't I – well maybe because they have wings

Why do people, in acceptance speeches, give God thanks and praise
  In certain churches, they shout and dance or their hands they raise

Why all the commotion, why can't they act more civilized
  Why can't they show composure, just looking for exposure, need to act
dignified

Why all the self-talks and self-reflection, why the words of affirmation
  Why all the extra fluff, all these so-called critical conversations
  May I offer a brief explanation?

If the space in which you live has placed you on a pedestal and at its center
  Has always confirmed the beauty of your existence and exalted you as
mankind's only winner

You would not understand the need to instill in one that their life truly
matters
  To mend broken spirits and minds that have been left in shreds and tatters

No need to remind your children of a legacy and existence stolen
  To reshape within their being an image that for our people will embolden

If you've never known deliverance or why a caged bird sings
This simple poem will not enlighten you to the crucial lessons of such things

But if you call yourself a Christian and Christ is the model for your life
The answer to these questions is simple, a quick look to Him should suffice

Therefore, if you sit in buildings called churches and claim to know that God is true
Then I pose this question, instead of questioning why we thank Him for all He's done, why don't you?

1 Thessalonians 5:18

Why Me

Swore I asked this long ago
   Back then I thought my gift a curse
   Only now beginning to understand
   You've anointed me, given me worth

Anytime something bad happened
   Anytime I felt any discomfort or fear
   There I would go questioning existence
   Mine and Yours, wondering why I am here

Questioning if You could hear me
   Doubtful if my problems mattered to You
   Lukewarm in my faith in me and my abilities
   Downright cold in my belief that You'd come through

Many years and tears have passed
   Through it all I continued to seek Your face
   Not sure what I was searching for at all
   Yet convinced it would lead me some place

Presented with questions, I had no answers
   I'm barely walking in my own belief
   Coming into the knowledge of my gift and purpose
   Brought me immense relief

Questions once a puzzle to me
    Not confounding me anymore
    Others may not want the answers
    Not quite what they're looking for

Asking why bad things happen
    To people that we consider "good"
    Interesting we don't use the word "blameless"
    Matters not, You do as You would

Asking "why me" in certain moments
    Poor us, so helpless we present
    Need to shake off the air of ignorance
    Seek the purpose for which we were meant

We always want from You
    Always expecting You to fix what we destroy
    Blame You for the mess that we create
    Then if You don't clean it up, then boy, oh boy

I ask "why me" as a humble question
    As I love You and appreciate Your gift
    You've given me a compassion for Your Children
    A spirit content to remember to lift

An ability to simplify some things
    And to make some things quite clear
    While we wait for You to do everything
    There is a reason that we are here

"Why me" is a question for all of us
    To humbly seek Your grace
    To build a relationship with You

And know why we live within this space

What is our specific purpose
    What is our unique role
    As we seek Your kingdom daily
    Your lessons and blessings will unfold

We tend to have things backwards
    We want you to come to us first
    Love living out of order
    Constantly making things worse

Took me long to figure out
    What my life was supposed to be
    Thank You, Lord for Your blessings
    And for answering when I asked, "why me"

James 1:5

Winner

Being a winner
  Not meant for a beginner

You'll waste the purpose
  Render it worthless

Too self-indulgent to notice
  Lost all your focus

Sacrifice peace for a high
  Never learned how to get by

Lonely and deserted
  Tried to warn you, but you'd heard it

A know-it-all who knows nothing
  Spending time needlessly suffering

It all came too fast
  It had no chance to last

Addicted to the power of it all
  Heavy was your fall

All those you trampled
  Even those you let sample

Feel pity and sorrow
  Hoping you'll get it – maybe, tomorrow

Without a care or a friend
  Wondering how it all came to an end

The winner never had a clue
  The winning was never about you

1 Corinthians 9:16-19, 22-24

World of Contradiction

Contradictions leading to conflicts
    Competing thoughts, no one predicts
    How, pray tell, will this all end?

Thought I had it right, but I was wrong
    Truth in front of us all along
    Yet not one of us is willing to bend.

The message seems contradictory
    For both of us it remains a great mystery
    Yet both of us sure we've figured it out.

This tug of war or war of the minds
    Bending of wills spanning all of time
    Still leaves many with shadows of doubt.

What's black is white, empty is full
    Light is dark, good is evil
    Love seems to never love in kind

We'll never see the world the same
    Don't care to know each other's name
    Opposing views make for closed minds.

Is there a path to set us right?
  We refuse to pause the fight
  To determine if there is room for common ground

Talking over one another
  Brother set against brother
  We are so lost; will we ever again be found?

Living in a world of contradictions
  Every man dug into their convictions
  No time to see through the eyes of love and realize

We are caught up in a contrived fight
  Yet, we fight with all our might.
  If your side wins the victory, what is the true prize?

1 Corinthians 13:9-12; James 4:1-2; Matthew 24:6

You Got Me

Bright lights shining
  I'm not opining
  You got me

They will criticize
  No surprise
  You got me

Some won't understand
  This is your plan
  You got me

They'll think it's about me
  You will help them see
  You got me

Fear will come
  Your will be done
  You got me

They'll deny
  I have to try
  You got me

Here come problems
    For You to solve them
    You got me

They're remarks will be brutal
    Yeah, but they will be futile
    Because You got me

Psalm 23

Mahogany Roots

What is it about the roots of a tree
  They nourish and repair and sustain me
  They make me stand straight when I think I'm not able
  The strength of my roots is what keeps me stable
  My roots are the anchor that hold me steady
  They have all that I need to ensure I am ready
  As a tree is known by the fruit it bears
  May I eat of its knowledge, but only my share
  And as seeds are planted inside of me
  May their roots take hold like a Mahogany tree

Jeremiah 17:8; Luke 6:43-45

Coming Soon Mahogany Roots Elementary Book Series

About the Author

Dr. Mary Giles Hanks is a native of York, Alabama. She is passionate about the education of young people and elevation of all people. Poetry is a means of telling stories and showing how faith, purpose, and everyday living are connected entities. Her love of humanity and obedience to submit to God's purpose for her life guides the storytelling. It also necessitates honoring the past, acknowledging the present, and preparing for the future. All of us have a story. These stories must be told by those who experience them through their unique perspective. Hopefully, Dr. Hanks' perspective will allow others to gain insight if they will listen to the stories with compassion and seek understanding, while forsaking judgment. More importantly, Dr. Hanks hopes to inspire, encourage, and challenge others to seek knowledge and truth. Dr. Hanks is the birth mother of two children, but through her work at the University of West Alabama Division of Nursing, she has many "children" in the world who are healing, nurturing, and building a legacy for future generations.